HEALTHY RECIPES

Publications International, Ltd.

Publications International, Ltd.

CONTENTS

Italian Eggplant with Millet
and Pepper Stuffing (page 62)

Delicious Pepper Steak
(page 142)

Hearty Lentil Stew
(page 82)

Asian Kale and Chickpeas (page 56)

HEALTHY EATING

Many families look for ways to balance their need to eat healthful, nutritious meals with their desire to eat the hearty, home-style food most familiar to them. This cookbook presents healthier versions of slow-cooked foods made in the **CROCK-POT**® slow cooker.

Eating together at home as a family can nurture relationships and promote quality time. In addition, cooking at home allows you to choose your ingredients and control your portions. The familiar, well-loved recipes in this cookbook prove that you can prepare and eat healthy foods without sacrificing good taste. Even better, you can count on your **CROCK-POT**® slow cooker to create the same time-tested, convenient and hassle-free meals it always has.

Whether you're embarking on a new healthy eating plan, or you're looking for some nutritious recipes to add to your repertoire, this cookbook has something for you. The recipes were selected to offer delicious, nutritionally balanced foods that cooks everywhere can confidently offer to their families.

The Principles of Healthy Eating

Whether you're trying to lose weight, maintain your weight or just eat better, basic nutrition information is what you need under your belt. It's easy to be led astray and ultimately become disappointed by misinformation and diets that make outrageous promises. That's why it is important to learn about the role of nutrients in food and how these nutrients are used in your body. Armed with this knowledge, you can resist the siren call of unhealthy diets and make an informed decision about a healthy eating plan that's right for you.

Nutrition Fundamentals

Most foods contain a combination of three energy-producing nutrients—protein, fat and carbohydrate. These nutrients are responsible for providing the energy that your body needs to run well and they are essential to your health. Your body requires all three, as well as vitamins, minerals and water. Fiber, a type of carbohydrate, and fluids both play important roles in managing your weight, too.

If you're trying to lose weight, you've certainly heard the word calorie. Basically, calorie is another word for energy. There are four sources of calories: the three energy-producing nutrients mentioned above (protein, fat and carbohydrate) and alcohol. Fiber, although it's a carbohydrate, is not processed by the body and is calorie-free.

Calorie Basics

Weight loss (and weight gain, for that matter) is primarily an issue of calories: how many you consume and how many you expend. If the number of calories you eat and the number of calories you use each day are approximately the same, your weight won't budge. It's only when you consume fewer calories than you use over a period of time that you will lose weight. And it's only when you eat more calories than you use that you will gain weight.

So what numbers of calories are we talking about? This is the crucial equation: One pound of body weight is equal to 3,500 calories. This means that to lose one pound, you must create a 3,500-calorie shortage by eating fewer calories, burning more calories through physical activity, or a combination of both. The exact opposite is true for weight gain. Sounds like a lot, doesn't it? But it's not really. Gaining a pound is as easy as eating an extra 250 calories a day (for instance, any of these: three chocolate chip cookies, one milk chocolate bar, two ounces Cheddar cheese or a medium-size bagel) for two weeks or skipping a daily workout without cutting back on eating.

And despite claims from popular diet plans, a calorie is a calorie, whether it comes from protein, fat or carbohydrate. Any calories eaten that your body doesn't burn for energy are stored as body fat, no matter what kind of food package they came in.

There are a few other factors, in addition to calories, that influence your weight. They are your age, your gender and your genetic blueprint. Unfortunately, these factors are out of your control. So focus on food intake and physical activity, the areas in which you can have an impact.

Making Smart Choices

Eating right and being physically active go hand in hand with keeping a healthy lifestyle. There are certain guidelines you should follow to keep on top of your healthy habits and reducing your risk of chronic diseases and obesity.

The best way to get a handle on eating right is to balance your meals by eating a variety of foods each day. Your goal should be to:

- Select lean sources of protein—like lean meats and poultry. Also add more fish, beans, legumes, and nuts for additional protein.
- Select fresh fruits and vegetables when you can. Opt for fresh, frozen, canned or dried fruits over fruit juices and choose more dark green or orange vegetables for added nutrition and increased fiber.
- Make half your grains whole. Choose whole grains when possible, when selecting cereals, breads, rice and pasta. Look for grains that say "whole grains" in the ingredient list. This will also be a fiber boost for you.
- Choose fat-free and low-fat milk and dairy products, like cheese and yogurt. These foods will provide you with all that great nutrition, but without excess fat.

- Know your limits. Look for foods that are low in saturated fats, trans fats, cholesterol, salt (sodium) and added sugars.

Each person should aim for a certain number of calories each day. This particular number is based on your age, sex, activity level and whether you are seeking to maintain your weight, gain weight or lose weight. Typically 2,000 calories is the general reference number used for the average adult to maintain their weight. If you are seeking to lose a few pounds, you will need to reduce this number of calories.

When choosing foods, whether they be those for meals or for snacks, you should seek out choices that are "nutrient dense" and not "empty-calorie" foods. In other words, you should choose foods that provide you the most nutrition for the number of calories (or food energy) that they provide. Choosing foods with calories as well as adequate vitamins and minerals would definitely be a better choice than one, like a sugary soft drink, that provides only calories from sugar, and no other nutrition value.

Now that you are focusing on the "better" food choices, you must also keep in mind the importance of portion sizes. Any food that is eaten in too large a quantity, even a good-for-you food, is not a good choice. In order to balance your meals, you should seek out the variety of foods you need, in recommended portion sizes. Refer to the charts on pages 8 and 9 for some examples and tips.

The Comfort of Food

The process of improving one's diet can seem fairly daunting, even frightening. We hear and see so many messages on the importance of a healthful diet that it's easy to feel overwhelmed by the decision of what to eat. Partly this is because many of the messages we receive about food conflict with one another. But another key factor is the role food plays in our lives.

On a certain level, food plays a basic functional role in our daily lives. There are plenty of scientific studies documenting how many calories a person needs each day, the best sources of those calories, the sorts of nutrients we need to ingest each day, etc. While we certainly need to fuel our bodies, food means much more to us than just fuel. Food provides a much needed emotional contact for most people. A shared breakfast, lunch or dinner is the centerpiece of many families' daily interactions with one another. Food comforts us in these and many other ways.

What Is Comfort Food?

When we connect with our loved ones over specific foods, those foods take on an emotional role of their own. That's why, even years later Grandma's special Sunday roast recipe reminds us of her and the good times we shared with the whole family. That's one of the most important ways certain foods, comfort foods especially, feed our emotional side in addition to our physical side.

For most Americans, "comfort foods" include many of the most classic sorts of **CROCK-POT®** slow cooker foods like pot roast, roasted chicken and potatoes, chicken soup and even spicier fare like chili. Unfortunately, some of the traditional

Choose Wisely

Eating the familiar, well-loved recipes in this cookbook can help you keep to a sensible eating plan. Consider the following ways to help create healthier versions of your own favorite **CROCK-POT®** slow cooker recipes.

In general
- Portion sizes are incredibly important. Don't be afraid to measure out portions with measuring cups or an accurate kitchen scale.
- Use high calorie or fatty ingredients sparingly or as garnish. Try sprinkling cheese on top of each serving, rather than adding cups of it into the recipe itself. You'll still get the flavor, but you'll avoid all of the fat.

Ingredients are important
- Recipes using leaner cuts of meat are great choices to start with. Look for recipes for skinless, boneless white meat cuts of poultry. Beef recipes made with cuts with "loin" or "round" in their names are also good options, as are pork recipes made with boneless "loin" cuts.
- Try substituting equal weights of these boneless cuts for bone-in or fattier cuts in your favorite recipes.

- Look for reduced-fat and reduced-sodium versions of other commonly used ingredients. For example, almost all of the canned broths and canned beans used in these recipes are either reduced-fat and/or reduced-sodium versions.
- Packaged and prepared products are convenient, but they are often the source of hidden salt or fat in recipes. Try fresh or frozen alternatives to boxed or canned versions whenever practical.

Relative Serving Sizes

There will be occasions when it may be difficult or impractical to measure your meals with a scale or measuring cups. Learning how to estimate appropriate serving sizes can be tricky, but it's made easier if you learn to approximate relative sizes like those in this list:

Fruits
1 cup cut-up fruit = closed fist
½ cup grapes or berries = light bulb
1 medium apple, orange, pear, etc. = baseball

Vegetables
1 cup baby carrots = tennis ball
1 medium ear of corn = as long as an unsharpened pencil
1 cup broccoli florets = rounded handful

Dairy
1 ounce firm cheese (like Cheddar) = 9-volt battery
1 cup yogurt or cottage cheese = closed fist
½ cup shredded cheese = enough to fill a typical paper cupcake liner

Proteins
3 ounces beef or pork = deck of cards or about the size of the palm of your hand
3 ounces chicken = average size chicken leg and thigh portion; small chicken breast
3 ounces grilled or baked fish fillet = checkbook

Grains and Starches
½ cup pasta or rice = typical scoop of ice cream
1 ounce bread = typical slice of sandwich bread
1 medium potato = computer mouse

ways of cooking these recipes rely on unhealthy levels of fat and sodium to create the great flavors we remember.

Comfort Food = Diet Food?

The recipes in this book were selected to have fewer calories, fat, sodium and cholesterol than typical recipes. Consider your own dietary needs and calorie allowance for the day when choosing recipes. Refer to the nutritional analysis and the icons after each recipe title, so you have the information to select the recipes that are appropriate for you.

With this cookbook it's simple to plan meals and budget your calories. For example, if you have a higher calorie lunch, select a dinner that's lower in calories to balance out your intake.

Whether you're trying to lose weight, hoping to prevent gaining additional weight or just

looking for ways to eat healthier, the recipes in this cookbook can provide you the heart-warming comfort of your favorite foods, without the fat and calories.

Nutritional Icons

HF **High Fiber** = 5g or more

LF **Low Fat** = 3g or less

LS **Low Salt** = 140mg or less

V **Vegetarian** = no meat products

GF **Gluten Free** = no wheat, rye or barley

Chipotle Vegetable Chili with Chocolate (page 88)

SLOW COOKING 101

Hints and Tips

CROCK-POT® Slow Cooker Sizes

Smaller slow cookers—such as 1- to 3½-quart models—are the perfect size for cooking for singles, a couple or empty-nesters (and also for serving dips).

While medium-size slow cookers (those holding somewhere between 3 quarts and 5 quarts) will easily cook enough food at a time to feed a small family, they're also convenient for holiday side dishes or appetizers.

Large slow cookers are great for large family dinners, holiday entertaining and potluck suppers. A 6- to 7-quart model is ideal if you like to make meals in advance, or have dinner tonight and store leftovers for another day.

Types of CROCK-POT® Slow Cookers

Current **CROCK-POT®** slow cookers come equipped with many different features and benefits, including auto cook programs and timed programming. Visit **www.crock-pot.com** to find the **CROCK-POT®** slow cooker that best suits your needs.

How you plan to use a **CROCK-POT®** slow cooker may affect the model you choose to purchase. For everyday cooking, choose a size large enough to serve your family. If you plan to use the **CROCK-POT®** slow cooker primarily for entertaining, choose one of the larger sizes. Basic **CROCK-POT®** slow cookers can hold as little as 16 ounces or as much as 7 quarts. The smallest sizes are great for keeping dips hot on a buffet, while the larger sizes can more readily fit large quantities of food and larger roasts.

Cooking, Stirring and Food Safety

CROCK-POT® slow cookers are safe to leave unattended. The outer heating base may get hot as it cooks, but it should not pose a fire hazard. The heating element in the heating base functions at a low wattage and is safe for your countertops.

Your **CROCK-POT®** slow cooker should be filled about one-half to three-fourths full for most recipes unless otherwise instructed. Lean meats such as chicken or pork tenderloin will cook faster than meats with more connective tissue and fat such as beef chuck or pork shoulder. Bone-in meats will take longer than boneless cuts. Typical **CROCK-POT**® slow cooker dishes take approximately 7 to 8 hours to reach the simmer point on LOW and about 3 to 4 hours on HIGH. Once the vegetables and meat start to simmer and braise, their flavors will fully blend and meat will become fall-off-the-bone tender.

According to the USDA, all bacteria are killed at a temperature of 165°F. It's important to follow the recommended cooking times and not to open the lid often, especially early in the cooking process when heat is building up inside the unit. If you need to open the lid to check on your food or are adding additional ingredients, remember to allow additional cooking time if necessary to ensure food is cooked through and tender.

Large **CROCK-POT**® slow cookers, the 6- to 7-quart sizes, may benefit from a quick stir halfway during cook time to help distribute heat and promote even cooking. It's usually unnecessary to stir at all, as even ½ cup liquid will help to distribute heat, and the stoneware is the perfect medium for holding food at an even temperature throughout the cooking process.

Oven-Safe

All **CROCK-POT**® slow cooker removable stoneware inserts may (without their lids) be used safely in ovens at up to 400°F. Also, all **CROCK-POT**® slow cookers are microwavable without their lids. If you own another brand slow cooker, please refer to your owner's manual for specific stoneware cooking medium tolerances.

Frozen Food

Frozen food or partially frozen food can be successfully cooked in a **CROCK-POT**® slow cooker; however, it will require longer cooking than the same recipe made with fresh food. It's almost always preferable to thaw frozen food prior to placing it in the **CROCK-POT**® slow cooker. Using an instant-read thermometer is recommended to ensure meat is fully cooked through.

Quinoa and Vegetable Medley (page 244)

Spinach and Ricotta Stuffed Shells (page 64)

Pasta and Rice

If you're converting a recipe that calls for uncooked pasta, cook the pasta on the stovetop just until slightly tender before adding to the **CROCK-POT**® slow cooker. If you are converting a recipe that calls for cooked rice, stir in raw rice with other ingredients; add ¼ cup extra liquid per ¼ cup of raw rice.

Beans

Beans must be softened completely before combining with sugar and/or acidic foods. Sugar and acid have a hardening effect on beans and will prevent softening. Fully cooked canned beans may be used as a substitute for dried beans.

Vegetables

Root vegetables often cook more slowly than meat. Cut vegetables accordingly to cook at the same rate as meat—large or small, or lean versus marbled—and place near the sides or bottom of the stoneware to facilitate cooking.

Herbs

Fresh herbs add flavor and color when added at the end of the cooking cycle; if added at the beginning, many fresh herbs' flavor will dissipate over long cook times. Ground and/or dried herbs and spices work well in slow cooking and may be added at the beginning, and for dishes with shorter cook times, hearty fresh herbs such as rosemary and thyme hold up well. The flavor power of all herbs and spices can vary greatly depending on their particular strength and shelf life. Use chili powders and garlic powder sparingly, as these can sometimes intensify over the long cook times. Always taste the dish at end of the cook cycle and correct seasonings including salt and pepper.

Vegetable Soup with Beans (page 83)

Liquids

It's not necessary to use more than ½ to 1 cup liquid in most instances since juices in meats and vegetables are retained more in slow cooking than in conventional cooking. Excess liquid can be cooked down and concentrated after slow cooking on the stovetop or by removing meat and vegetables from the stoneware, stirring in one of the following thickeners and setting the **CROCK-POT®** slow cooker to HIGH. Cover; cook on HIGH for approximately 15 minutes until juices are thickened.

Flour: All-purpose flour is often used to thicken soups or stews. Place flour in a small bowl or cup and stir in enough cold water to make a thin, lump-free mixture. With the **CROCK-POT®** slow cooker on HIGH, quickly whisk the flour mixture into the liquid in the **CROCK-POT®** slow cooker. Cover; cook on HIGH until the mixture thickens.

Cornstarch: Cornstarch gives sauces a clear, shiny appearance; it's used most often for sweet dessert sauces and stir-fry sauces. Place cornstarch in a small bowl or cup and stir in cold water until the cornstarch dissolves. Quickly whisk this mixture into the liquid in the **CROCK-POT®** slow cooker; the sauce will thicken as soon as the liquid simmers. Cornstarch breaks down with too much heat, so never add it at the beginning of the slow cooking process, and turn off the heat as soon as the sauce thickens.

Arrowroot: Arrowroot (or arrowroot flour) comes from the root of a tropical plant that is dried and ground to a powder; it produces a thick, clear sauce. Those who are allergic to wheat often use it in place of flour. Place arrowroot in a small bowl or cup and stir in cold water until the mixture is smooth. Quickly whisk this mixture into the liquid in the **CROCK-POT®** slow cooker. Arrowroot thickens below the boiling point, so it works well in the **CROCK-POT®** slow cooker on LOW. Too much stirring can break down an arrowroot mixture.

Tapioca: Tapioca is a starchy substance extracted from the root of the cassava plant. Its greatest advantage is that it withstands long cooking, making it an ideal choice for slow cooking. Add it at the beginning of cooking and you'll get a clear, thickened sauce in the finished dish. Dishes using tapioca as a thickener are best cooked on the LOW setting; tapioca may become stringy when heated for a long time.

Milk

Milk, cream and sour cream break down during extended cooking. When possible, add during the last 15 to 30 minutes of cooking, just until heated through. Condensed soups may be substituted for milk and can cook for an extended time.

Fish

Fish is delicate and should be added during the last 15 to 30 minutes of cooking time. Cook until just cooked through and serve immediately.

Baked Goods

If you wish to prepare bread, cakes or pudding cakes in a **CROCK-POT**® slow cooker, you may want to purchase a covered, vented metal cake pan accessory for your **CROCK-POT**® slow cooker. You can also use any straight-sided soufflé dish or deep cake pan that will fit into the stoneware insert of your unit. Baked goods can be prepared directly in the insert; however, they can be a little difficult to remove from the insert, so follow the recipe directions carefully.

Bran Muffin Bread (page 20)

WHOLESOME BREAKFAST

Bacon and Cheese Brunch Potatoes GF

- **3 medium russet potatoes (about 2 pounds), cut into 1-inch cubes**
- **1 cup chopped onion**
- **½ teaspoon seasoned salt**
- **4 slices bacon, crisp-cooked and crumbled**
- **1 cup (4 ounces) shredded sharp Cheddar cheese**
- **1 tablespoon water**

1. Coat inside of **CROCK-POT**® slow cooker with nonstick cooking spray. Place half of potatoes in **CROCK-POT**® slow cooker. Sprinkle half of onion and seasoned salt over potatoes; top with half of bacon and cheese. Repeat layers, ending with cheese. Sprinkle water over top.

2. Cover; cook on LOW 6 hours or on HIGH 3½ hours. Stir gently to mix; serve warm.

Makes 6 servings

Nutrition Information:
Serving Size about 1 cup, **Calories** 197, **Total Fat** 8g, **Saturated Fat** 4g, **Protein** 9g, **Carbohydrate** 22g, **Cholesterol** 26mg, **Dietary Fiber** 2g, **Sodium** 379mg

Broccoli and Cheese Strata Ⓥ

- **2 cups chopped broccoli florets**
- **4 slices firm white bread, ½ inch thick**
- **1 tablespoon unsalted butter**
- **1 cup (4 ounces) shredded Cheddar cheese**
- **1½ cups fat-free (skim) milk**
- **2 eggs**
- **2 egg whites**
- **½ teaspoon salt**
- **½ teaspoon hot pepper sauce**
- **⅛ teaspoon black pepper**
- **1 cup water**

1. Spray 1-quart casserole or soufflé dish that fits inside of 2½- to 3-quart **CROCK-POT®** slow cooker with nonstick cooking spray. Fill large saucepan with water; bring to a boil. Add broccoli; cook 5 minutes or until tender. Drain.

2. Spread one side of each bread slice with butter. Arrange 2 slices bread, buttered sides up, in prepared casserole. Layer cheese, broccoli and remaining 2 bread slices, buttered sides down. Whisk milk, eggs, egg whites, salt, hot pepper sauce and black pepper in medium bowl; slowly pour over bread.

3. Place small wire rack in **CROCK-POT®** slow cooker. Pour in 1 cup water. Place casserole on rack. Cover; cook on HIGH 3 hours. Cut strata evenly into four wedges.

Makes 4 servings

Nutrition Information:
Serving Size 1 wedge, **Calories** 201, **Total Fat** 8g, **Saturated Fat** 4g, **Protein** 13g, **Carbohydrate** 20g, **Cholesterol** 91mg, **Dietary Fiber** 1g, **Sodium** 618mg

Bran Muffin Bread

- **2 cups all-bran cereal**
- **2 cups whole wheat flour***
- **2 teaspoons baking powder**
- **1 teaspoon baking soda**
- **½ teaspoon salt**
- **¼ teaspoon ground cinnamon**
- **1 egg**
- **1½ cups buttermilk**
- **¼ cup molasses**
- **¼ cup (½ stick) unsalted butter, melted**
- **1 cup chopped walnuts**
- **½ cup raisins**
- **Prepared honey butter (optional)**

TIP

Cooking times are guidelines. CROCK-POT® slow cookers, just like ovens, cook differently depending on the recipe size and the individual CROCK-POT® slow cooker. Always check for doneness before serving.

For proper texture of finished bread, spoon flour into measuring cup and level off. Do not dip into bag, pack down flour or tap on counter to level.

1. Butter and flour 8-cup mold that fits inside 6-quart **CROCK-POT**® slow cooker. Combine cereal, flour, baking powder, baking soda, salt and cinnamon in large bowl.

2. Beat egg in medium bowl. Whisk in buttermilk, molasses and melted butter. Stir into flour mixture just until combined. Stir in walnuts and raisins. Spoon batter into prepared mold. Cover with buttered foil, butter side down.

3. Place rack in **CROCK-POT**® slow cooker. Pour 1 inch hot water into **CROCK-POT**® slow cooker (water should not come to top of rack). Place mold on rack. Cover; cook on LOW 3½ to 4 hours or until bread starts to pull away from side of mold and toothpick inserted into center comes out clean. (If necessary, replace foil. Cover; cook on LOW 45 minutes.)

4. Remove mold from **CROCK-POT**® slow cooker. Let stand 10 minutes. Remove foil and run rubber spatula around outer edge, lifting bottom slightly to loosen. Invert bread onto wire rack; cut evenly into 12 slices. Serve warm with honey butter, if desired.

Makes 1 loaf

Nutrition Information:
Serving Size 1 slice, **Calories** 258, **Total Fat** 12g, **Saturated Fat** 4g, **Protein** 8g, **Carbohydrate** 36g, **Cholesterol** 31mg, **Dietary Fiber** 6g, **Sodium** 356mg

Apple-Cinnamon Breakfast Risotto LS V GF

3 tablespoons unsalted butter

4 medium Granny Smith apples (about 1½ pounds), peeled and cut into ½-inch cubes

1½ teaspoons ground cinnamon

¼ teaspoon ground allspice

¼ teaspoon salt

1½ cups uncooked Arborio rice

½ cup packed dark brown sugar

4 cups unfiltered apple juice, at room temperature*

1 teaspoon vanilla

Optional toppings: dried cranberries, sliced almonds and/or milk

*If unfiltered apple juice is unavailable, use any apple juice.

TIP

Keep the lid on! The CROCK-POT® slow cooker can take as long as 30 minutes to regain heat lost when the cover is removed.

1. Coat inside of **CROCK-POT®** slow cooker with nonstick cooking spray. Melt butter in large skillet over medium-high heat. Add apples, cinnamon, allspice and salt; cook and stir 3 to 5 minutes or until apples begin to release juices. Remove to **CROCK-POT®** slow cooker.

2. Stir in rice and sprinkle evenly with brown sugar. Add apple juice and vanilla. Cover; cook on HIGH 1½ to 2 hours or until all liquid is absorbed. Top as desired.

Makes 6 servings

Nutrition Information:
Serving Size 1¼ cups, **Calories** 342, **Total Fat** 6g, **Saturated Fat** 4g, **Protein** 2g, **Carbohydrate** 72g, **Cholesterol** 15mg, **Dietary Fiber** 4g, **Sodium** 123mg

Apple-Cranberry Crêpes

- **1** baking apple, such as Gala or Jonathan, peeled, cored and cut into 6 wedges
- **1** tart apple, such as Granny Smith, peeled, cored and cut into 6 wedges
- **¼** cup dried sweetened cranberries or cherries
- **2** tablespoons lemon juice
- **½** teaspoon plus ⅛ teaspoon ground cinnamon, divided
- **⅛** teaspoon ground nutmeg
- **⅛** teaspoon ground cloves or allspice
- **1** tablespoon butter
- **¼** cup orange juice
- **1** tablespoon sugar substitute
- **¾** teaspoon cornstarch
- **¼** teaspoon almond extract
- **4** prepared crêpes
- **1** cup no-sugar-added reduced-fat vanilla ice cream (optional)

Look for prepared crêpes in the produce section of the supermarket.

1. Coat inside of **CROCK-POT**® slow cooker with nonstick cooking spray. Place apples, cranberries, lemon juice, ½ teaspoon cinnamon, nutmeg and cloves in **CROCK-POT**® slow cooker; toss to coat. Cover; cook on LOW 2 hours. Stir butter into apple mixture just until melted.

2. Stir orange juice, sugar substitute, cornstarch and almond extract in small bowl until cornstarch dissolves. Stir into apple mixture in **CROCK-POT**® slow cooker. Turn **CROCK-POT**® slow cooker to HIGH. Cover; cook on HIGH 15 minutes or until sauce thickens slightly.

3. Place 1 crêpe on each of four dessert plates. Spoon apple mixture evenly down center of each crêpe. Fold edges over; turn crêpes with seam side down on plates. Sprinkle with remaining ⅛ teaspoon cinnamon. Microwave filled crêpes according to package directions, if desired. Serve with ice cream, if desired.

Makes 4 servings

Nutrition Information:
Serving Size 1 crêpe with 3 apple wedges and about 1 tablespoon sauce, **Calories** 235, **Total Fat** 9g, **Saturated Fat** 2g, **Protein** 6g, **Carbohydrate** 34g, **Cholesterol** 101mg, **Dietary Fiber** 3g, **Sodium** 221mg

Raisin-Oat Quick Bread ⓥ

⅔ **cup old-fashioned oats**

⅓ **cup fat-free (skim) milk**

1½ **cups all-purpose flour, plus additional for dusting**

4 **teaspoons baking powder**

1 **teaspoon ground cinnamon**

½ **teaspoon salt**

½ **cup packed raisins**

1 **cup sugar**

2 **eggs, slightly beaten**

½ **cup (1 stick) unsalted butter, melted, plus additional for serving**

1 **teaspoon vanilla**

1. Spray inside of ovenproof glass or ceramic loaf pan that fits inside **CROCK-POT**® slow cooker with nonstick cooking spray; dust with flour.

2. Combine oats and milk in small bowl; let stand 10 minutes.

3. Meanwhile, combine 1½ cups flour, baking powder, cinnamon and salt in large bowl; stir in raisins. Whisk sugar, eggs, butter and vanilla in separate medium bowl; stir in oat mixture. Pour sugar mixture into flour mixture; stir just until moistened. Pour into prepared pan. Place in **CROCK-POT**® slow cooker. Cover; cook on HIGH 2½ to 3 hours or until toothpick inserted into center comes out clean.

4. Remove bread from **CROCK-POT**® slow cooker; let cool in pan 10 minutes. Remove bread from pan; let cool on wire rack 3 minutes before evenly cutting into 12 slices. Serve with additional butter, if desired.

Makes 1 loaf

Nutrition Information:
Serving Size 1 slice, **Calories** 240, **Total Fat** 9g, **Saturated Fat** 5g, **Protein** 4g, **Carbohydrate** 38g, **Cholesterol** 50mg, **Dietary Fiber** 1g, **Sodium** 250mg

Roasted Pepper and Sourdough Egg Dish

- **3** cups sourdough bread cubes
- **1** jar (12 ounces) roasted red pepper strips, drained
- **1** cup (4 ounces) shredded reduced-fat Monterey Jack cheese
- **1** cup (4 ounces) shredded reduced-fat sharp Cheddar cheese
- **1** cup fat-free cottage cheese
- **1½** cups cholesterol-free egg substitute
- **1** cup fat-free (skim) milk
- **¼** cup chopped fresh cilantro
- **¼** teaspoon black pepper

1. Coat inside of **CROCK-POT**® slow cooker with nonstick cooking spray. Add bread. Arrange roasted peppers evenly over bread cubes; sprinkle with Monterey Jack and Cheddar cheeses.

2. Place cottage cheese in food processor or blender; process until smooth. Add egg substitute and milk; process just until blended. Stir in cilantro and black pepper.

3. Pour egg mixture into **CROCK-POT**® slow cooker. Cover; cook on LOW 3 to 3½ hours or on HIGH 2 to 2½ hours or until eggs are firm but still moist.

Makes 8 servings

Nutrition Information:
Serving Size ¾ cup, **Calories** 179, **Total Fat** 6g, **Saturated Fat** 3g, **Protein** 19g, **Carbohydrate** 13g, **Cholesterol** 22mg, **Dietary Fiber** 1g, **Sodium** 704mg

Oatmeal with Maple-Glazed Apples and Cranberries 🆑 🆅

3 **cups water**

2 **cups quick-cooking or old-fashioned oats**

¼ **teaspoon salt**

1 **teaspoon unsalted butter**

2 **medium red or Golden Delicious apples, unpeeled and cut into ½-inch pieces**

¼ **teaspoon ground cinnamon**

2 **tablespoons sugar-free maple syrup**

4 **tablespoons dried cranberries**

1. Combine water, oats and salt in **CROCK-POT**® slow cooker. Cover; cook on LOW 8 hours.

2. Melt butter in large nonstick skillet over medium heat. Add apples and cinnamon; cook and stir 4 to 5 minutes or until tender. Stir in syrup; heat through. Serve oatmeal with apple mixture and dried cranberries.

Makes 4 servings

Nutrition Information:
Serving Size ¾ cup oatmeal, ⅓ cup apple mixture and 1 tablespoon cranberries, **Calories** 230, **Total Fat** 4g, **Saturated Fat** 1g, **Protein** 6g, **Carbohydrate** 47g, **Cholesterol** 3mg, **Dietary Fiber** 6g, **Sodium** 158mg

Blueberry-Banana Pancakes ⓥ

  2 **cups all-purpose flour**

⅓ **cup sugar**

  1 **tablespoon baking powder**

½ **teaspoon baking soda**

½ **teaspoon salt**

½ **teaspoon ground cinnamon**

1¾ **cups fat-free (skim) milk**

  2 **eggs, lightly beaten**

¼ **cup (½ stick) unsalted butter, melted**

  1 **teaspoon vanilla**

  1 **cup fresh blueberries**

  2 **small bananas, sliced (optional)**

   Sugar-free maple syrup (optional)

1. Combine flour, sugar, baking powder, baking soda, salt and cinnamon in medium bowl. Combine milk, eggs, butter and vanilla in separate medium bowl. Pour milk mixture into flour mixture; stir until moistened. Gently fold in blueberries until combined.

2. Coat inside of **CROCK-POT**® slow cooker with nonstick cooking spray. Add batter to **CROCK-POT**® slow cooker. Cover; cook on HIGH 2 hours or until puffed and toothpick inserted into center comes out clean. Cut evenly into eight wedges; top with bananas and maple syrup, if desired.

Makes 8 servings

Nutrition Information:
Serving Size 1 wedge, **Calories** 240, **Total Fat** 7g, **Saturated Fat** 4g, **Protein** 7g, **Carbohydrate** 38g, **Cholesterol** 65mg, **Dietary Fiber** 1g, **Sodium** 270mg

4-Fruit Oatmeal ⓛⓕ ⓗⓕ ⓥ

4¼ cups water

1 cup steel-cut oats

¼ cup golden raisins

¼ cup dried cranberries

¼ cup dried cherries

2 tablespoons honey

1 teaspoon vanilla

¼ teaspoon salt

1 cup sliced fresh strawberries (optional)

Combine water, oats, raisins, cranberries, cherries, honey, vanilla and salt in **CROCK-POT®** slow cooker; stir to blend. Cover; cook on LOW 7 to 7½ hours. Top each serving evenly with strawberries, if desired.

Makes 4 servings

Nutrition Information:
Serving Size ½ cup
Calories 260
Total Fat 3g
Saturated Fat 1g
Protein 6g
Carbohydrate 53g
Cholesterol 0mg
Dietary Fiber 5g
Sodium 150mg

Cinnamon Latte Ⓛ Ⓥ Ⓖ

> **6** cups double-strength brewed coffee*
>
> **2** cups half-and-half
>
> **1** cup sugar
>
> **1** teaspoon vanilla
>
> **1½** teaspoons ground cinnamon
>
> Whipped cream and cinnamon sticks (optional)

Double the amount of coffee grounds normally used to brew coffee. Or, substitute 8 teaspoons instant coffee dissolved in 6 cups boiling water.

Combine coffee, half-and-half, sugar and vanilla in 3- to 4-quart **CROCK-POT**® slow cooker; stir to blend. Add ground cinnamon. Cover; cook on HIGH 3 hours. Garnish with whipped cream and cinnamon sticks.

Makes 8 servings

Nutrition Information:
Serving Size 1 cup
Calories 180
Total Fat 7g
Saturated Fat 4g
Protein 2g
Carbohydrate 28g
Cholesterol 22mg
Dietary Fiber 0g
Sodium 29mg

Mediterranean Frittata Ⓥ ⒼⒻ

- 3 tablespoons extra virgin olive oil
- 1 large onion, chopped
- 2 cups (about 8 ounces) sliced mushrooms
- 6 cloves garlic, sliced
- 1 teaspoon dried basil
- 1 medium red bell pepper, chopped
- 1 package (10 ounces) frozen chopped spinach, thawed and squeezed dry
- ¼ cup sliced kalamata olives
- 8 eggs, beaten
- 4 ounces feta cheese, crumbled
- ¼ teaspoon black pepper

1. Coat inside of **CROCK-POT**® slow cooker with nonstick cooking spray. Heat oil in large skillet over medium-high heat. Add onion, mushrooms, garlic and basil; cook and stir 2 to 3 minutes or until slightly softened. Add bell pepper; cook 4 to 5 minutes or until vegetables are tender. Stir in spinach; cook 2 minutes. Stir in olives. Remove onion mixture to **CROCK-POT**® slow cooker.

2. Combine eggs, cheese and black pepper in large bowl. Pour over vegetables in **CROCK-POT**® slow cooker. Cover; cook on LOW 2½ to 3 hours or on HIGH 1¼ to 1½ hours or until eggs are set. Cut evenly into eight wedges to serve.

Makes 8 servings

Nutrition Information:
Serving Size 1 wedge, **Calories** 220, **Total Fat** 16g, **Saturated Fat** 5g, **Protein** 11g, **Carbohydrate** 7g, **Cholesterol** 200mg, **Dietary Fiber** 2g, **Sodium** 440mg

Black Bean and Mushroom Chilaquiles

- **2** tablespoons olive oil
- **1** medium yellow onion, chopped
- **1** medium green bell pepper, chopped
- **1** jalapeño pepper, seeded and minced*
- **2** cans (about 15 ounces *each*) black beans, rinsed and drained
- **1** can (about 14 ounces) diced tomatoes
- **10** ounces white mushrooms, cut into quarters
- **1½** teaspoons ground cumin
- **1½** teaspoons dried oregano
- **1** cup (4 ounces) shredded sharp white Cheddar cheese, plus additional for garnish
- **6** cups baked corn tortilla chips, coarsely crushed

*Jalapeño peppers can sting and irritate the skin, so wear rubber gloves when handling peppers and do not touch your eyes.

1. Heat oil in medium skillet over medium heat. Add onion, bell pepper and jalapeño pepper; cook and stir 3 to 5 minutes or until onion is tender. Remove to **CROCK-POT®** slow cooker. Add beans, tomatoes, mushrooms, cumin and oregano. Cover; cook on LOW 6 hours or on HIGH 3 hours.

2. Sprinkle 1 cup cheese over beans and mushrooms. Cover; cook on HIGH 15 minutes or until cheese is melted. Stir to blend. Place 1 cup tortilla chips into each serving bowl. Top with black bean mixture. Garnish with additional cheese.

Makes 6 servings

Nutrition Information:
Serving Size 1½ cups bean mixture with 1 cup chips, **Calories** 347, **Total Fat** 11g, **Saturated Fat** 3g, **Protein** 14g, **Carbohydrate** 49g, **Cholesterol** 10mg, **Dietary Fiber** 9g, **Sodium** 755mg

Sausage and Red Pepper Strata

Nonstick cooking spray

12 **ounces reduced-fat bulk pork breakfast sausage**

1 **teaspoon dried oregano**

½ **teaspoon red pepper flakes (optional)**

8 **slices day-old French bread, cut into ½-inch cubes**

1 **medium red bell pepper, finely chopped**

¼ **cup chopped fresh Italian parsley, plus additional for garnish**

2 **cups cholesterol-free egg substitute**

2 **cups evaporated fat-free milk**

2 **teaspoons Dijon mustard**

½ **teaspoon black pepper**

1 **cup (4 ounces) shredded reduced-fat sharp Cheddar cheese**

1. Spray large skillet with cooking spray; heat over medium-high heat. Add sausage, oregano and red pepper flakes, if desired; cook 6 to 8 minutes or until browned, stirring to break up meat. Drain fat.

2. Coat inside of **CROCK-POT**® slow cooker with cooking spray. Add bread. Sprinkle sausage mixture evenly over bread; top with bell pepper and ¼ cup parsley.

3. Whisk egg substitute, evaporated milk, mustard and black pepper in medium bowl until well blended. Pour evenly over sausage mixture in **CROCK-POT**® slow cooker. Cover; cook on LOW 3 to 3½ hours or on HIGH 2 to 2½ hours or until eggs are firm but still moist.

4. Sprinkle cheese over top. Turn off heat. Cover; let stand 5 minutes or until cheese is melted. Cut evenly into eight squares. Garnish with additional parsley.

Makes 8 servings

Nutrition Information:
Serving Size 1 square, **Calories** 298, **Total Fat** 12g, **Saturated Fat** 2g, **Protein** 25g, **Carbohydrate** 23g, **Cholesterol** 43mg, **Dietary Fiber** 1g, **Sodium** 719mg

Breakfast Quinoa 🅛🅕 🅛🅢 🆅 🅖🅕

1½ **cups uncooked quinoa**

3 **cups water**

3 **tablespoons packed brown sugar**

2 **tablespoons maple syrup**

1½ **teaspoons ground cinnamon**

¾ **cup golden raisins**

Fresh raspberries and banana slices (optional)

1. Place quinoa in fine-mesh strainer; rinse well under cold running water. Remove to **CROCK-POT**® slow cooker.

2. Stir water, brown sugar, syrup and cinnamon into **CROCK-POT**® slow cooker. Cover; cook on LOW 5 hours or on HIGH 2½ hours or until quinoa is tender and water is absorbed.

3. Add raisins, if desired, during last 10 to 15 minutes of cooking time. Top each serving evenly with raspberries and bananas, if desired.

Makes 6 servings

Nutrition Information:
Serving Size ⅔ cup, **Calories** 233, **Total Fat** 3g, **Saturated Fat** 1g, **Protein** 6g, **Carbohydrate** 47g, **Cholesterol** 0mg, **Dietary Fiber** 4g, **Sodium** 9mg

Hawaiian Fruit Compote (LF) (HF) (LS) (V)

- 3 cups coarsely chopped fresh pineapple
- 3 grapefruits, peeled and sectioned
- 1 can (21 ounces) cherry pie filling
- 2 cups chopped fresh peaches
- 2 to 3 limes, peeled and sectioned
- 1 mango, peeled and chopped
- 2 bananas, sliced
- 1 tablespoon lemon juice
- Waffles or pancakes (optional)
- Slivered almonds (optional)

TIP

Warm, fruity compote makes a great substitute for maple syrup on your favorite pancakes and/or waffles.

Place pineapple, grapefruits, pie filling, peaches, limes, mango, bananas and lemon juice in **CROCK-POT®** slow cooker; toss lightly. Cover; cook on LOW 4 to 5 hours or on HIGH 2 to 3 hours. Serve over waffles, if desired. Garnish with almonds.

Makes 8 servings

Nutrition Information:
Serving Size 1 cup, **Calories** 225, **Total Fat** 0g, **Saturated Fat** 0g, **Protein** 2g, **Carbohydrate** 58g, **Cholesterol** 0mg, **Dietary Fiber** 8g, **Sodium** 15mg

MEATLESS MONDAYS

Cran-Orange Acorn Squash LF LS V GF

 5 **tablespoons instant brown rice**

 3 **tablespoons minced onion**

 3 **tablespoons diced celery**

 3 **tablespoons dried cranberries**

    Pinch ground sage

 3 **small acorn or carnival squash, cut in half and seeded**

 1 **teaspoon unsalted butter, cubed**

 9 **teaspoons orange juice**

 ½ **cup warm water**

1. Combine rice, onion, celery, cranberries and sage in small bowl. Stuff each squash halve with rice mixture; dot with butter. Pour 1½ teaspoons orange juice into each squash halve over stuffing.

2. Stand squash in **CROCK-POT**® slow cooker. Pour water into bottom of **CROCK-POT**® slow cooker. Cover; cook on LOW 2½ hours or until squash are tender.

Makes 6 servings

Nutrition Information:
Serving Size ½ squash with about ¼ cup stuffing, **Calories** 130, **Total Fat** 1g, **Saturated Fat** 0g, **Protein** 2g, **Carbohydrate** 30g, **Cholesterol** 0mg, **Dietary Fiber** 4g, **Sodium** 10mg

Vegetarian Lasagna

1 eggplant, sliced into ½-inch rounds

½ teaspoon salt

3 tablespoons olive oil, divided

1 medium zucchini, thinly sliced

8 ounces mushrooms, sliced

1 small onion, diced

1 can (26 ounces) reduced-sodium pasta sauce

1 teaspoon dried basil

1 teaspoon dried oregano

2 cups fat-free ricotta cheese

1½ cups (6 ounces) shredded reduced-fat mozzarella cheese

1 cup grated reduced-sodium Parmesan cheese, divided

1 package (8 ounces) whole-wheat lasagna noodles, cooked and drained

1. Sprinkle eggplant with salt; let stand 10 to 15 minutes. Rinse off excess salt and pat dry; brush with 1 tablespoon oil. Heat large skillet over medium heat. Add eggplant; cook 3 to 5 minutes or until browned on both sides. Remove to large paper towel-lined plate. Heat 1 tablespoon oil in same skillet over medium heat. Add zucchini; cook 3 to 5 minutes or until browned on both sides. Remove to separate large paper towel-lined plate.

2. Heat remaining 1 tablespoon oil in same skillet over medium heat; cook and stir mushrooms and onion until softened. Stir in pasta sauce, basil and oregano. Combine ricotta cheese, mozzarella cheese and ½ cup Parmesan cheese in medium bowl.

3. Spread ⅓ sauce mixture in bottom of **CROCK-POT**® slow cooker. Layer with ⅓ lasagna noodles, ½ eggplant, ½ cheese mixture. Repeat layers. For last layer, use remaining ⅓ of lasagna noodles, zucchini, remaining ⅓ of sauce mixture and top with remaining ½ cup Parmesan cheese.

4. Cover; cook on LOW 6 hours. Turn off heat. Let stand 15 to 20 minutes before evenly cutting into eight squares.

Makes 8 servings

Nutrition Information:
Serving Size 1 square, **Calories** 370, **Total Fat** 13g, **Saturated Fat** 5g, **Protein** 24g, **Carbohydrate** 38g, **Cholesterol** 25mg, **Dietary Fiber** 7g, **Sodium** 390mg

Bean and Vegetable Burritos

2 tablespoons chili powder

2 teaspoons dried oregano

1½ teaspoons ground cumin

1 large sweet potato, diced

1 can (about 15 ounces) black beans, rinsed and drained

4 cloves garlic, minced

1 medium yellow onion, halved and thinly sliced

1 jalapeño pepper, seeded and minced*

1 green bell pepper, chopped

1 cup frozen corn

3 tablespoons lime juice

1 tablespoon chopped fresh cilantro

¾ cup (3 ounces) shredded Monterey Jack cheese

6 (10-inch) flour tortillas, warmed

*Jalapeño peppers can sting and irritate the skin, so wear rubber gloves when handling peppers and do not touch your eyes.

1. Combine chili powder, oregano and cumin in small bowl. Layer sweet potato, beans, half of chili powder mixture, garlic, onion, jalapeño pepper, bell pepper, remaining half of chili powder mixture and corn in **CROCK-POT®** slow cooker. Cover; cook on LOW 5 hours or until sweet potato is tender. Stir in lime juice and cilantro.

2. Spoon 2 tablespoons cheese into center of each tortilla. Top with 1 cup filling. Fold up bottom edge of tortilla over filling; fold in sides and roll to enclose filling.

Makes 6 servings

 Nutrition Information:
Serving Size 1 burrito, **Calories** 392, **Total Fat** 11g, **Saturated Fat** 4g, **Protein** 14g, **Carbohydrate** 60g, **Cholesterol** 15mg, **Dietary Fiber** 8g, **Sodium** 800mg

Vegetarian Paella **HF** **V**

2 tablespoons olive oil

1 medium yellow onion, chopped

1 medium red bell pepper, chopped

2 cloves garlic, minced

1½ cups uncooked converted rice

2 cans (about 14 ounces *each*) reduced-sodium vegetable broth

½ cup dry white wine

½ teaspoon crushed saffron threads, smoked paprika or ground turmeric

¾ teaspoon salt

¼ teaspoon red pepper flakes

1 can (about 15 ounces) chickpeas, rinsed and drained

1 package (11 ounces) frozen artichoke hearts, thawed

½ cup frozen peas, thawed

1. Heat oil in medium skillet over medium heat. Add onion, bell pepper and garlic; cook and stir until onion is softened. Remove to **CROCK-POT**® slow cooker. Add rice, broth, wine, saffron, salt and red pepper flakes. Stir to level rice. Cover; cook on LOW 3 hours.

2. Add chickpeas, artichoke hearts and peas to **CROCK-POT**® slow cooker; do not stir. Cover; cook on LOW 30 minutes or until rice is tender and liquid is absorbed. Stir well just before serving.

Makes 6 servings

Nutrition Information:
Serving Size 2 cups, **Calories** 375, **Total Fat** 7g, **Saturated Fat** 1g, **Protein** 9g, **Carbohydrate** 65g, **Cholesterol** 0mg, **Dietary Fiber** 8g, **Sodium** 634mg

Vegetable Pasta Sauce 🅛🅕 🅗🅕 🅥

- **2** cans (about 14 ounces *each*) diced tomatoes
- **1** can (about 14 ounces) whole tomatoes, undrained
- **1½** cups sliced mushrooms
- **1** medium red bell pepper, chopped
- **1** medium green bell pepper, chopped
- **1** small yellow squash, cut into ¼-inch slices
- **1** small zucchini, cut into ¼-inch slices
- **1** can (6 ounces) tomato paste
- **4** green onions, sliced
- **3** cloves garlic, minced
- **2** tablespoons Italian seasoning
- **1** tablespoon chopped fresh Italian parsley
- **1** teaspoon red pepper flakes (optional)
- **1** teaspoon black pepper
- **2** cups hot cooked pasta
  Parmesan cheese and fresh basil leaves (optional)

Combine tomatoes, mushrooms, bell peppers, squash, zucchini, tomato paste, green onions, garlic, Italian seasoning, parsley, red pepper flakes, if desired, and black pepper in **CROCK-POT®** slow cooker; stir to blend. Cover; cook on LOW 6 to 8 hours. Serve over pasta. Top with cheese and basil, if desired.

Makes 6 servings

Nutrition Information:
Serving Size 2 cups sauce over ¼ cup pasta, **Calories** 370, **Total Fat** 2g, **Saturated Fat** 0g, **Protein** 15g, **Carbohydrate** 77g, **Cholesterol** 0mg, **Dietary Fiber** 8g, **Sodium** 660mg

Asian Kale and Chickpeas HF V

1 tablespoon sesame oil

1 medium onion, thinly sliced

2 teaspoons grated fresh ginger

2 cloves garlic, minced

2 jalapeño peppers, chopped*

8 cups chopped kale

1 cup reduced-sodium vegetable broth

2 cans (about 15 ounces *each*) unsalted chickpeas, rinsed and drained

1 tablespoon lime juice

1 teaspoon grated lime peel

2 cups hot cooked rice (optional)

Jalapeño peppers can sting and irritate the skin, so wear rubber gloves when handling peppers and do not touch your eyes.

1. Coat inside of **CROCK-POT**® slow cooker with nonstick cooking spray. Heat oil in large skillet over medium-high heat. Add onion, ginger, garlic and jalapeño peppers; cook 1 minute. Add kale; cook and stir 2 minutes or until slightly wilted. Remove kale mixture to **CROCK-POT**® slow cooker. Add broth and chickpeas.

2. Cover; cook on LOW 3 hours. Turn off heat. Stir in lime juice and lime peel. Serve with rice, if desired.

Makes 4 servings

Nutrition Information:
Serving Size 1¾ cups, **Calories** 330, **Total Fat** 6g, **Saturated Fat** 1g, **Protein** 18g, **Carbohydrate** 56g, **Cholesterol** 0mg, **Dietary Fiber** 13g, **Sodium** 370mg

Vegetable Curry

- **4** baking potatoes, chopped
- **1** large yellow onion, chopped
- **1** red bell pepper, chopped
- **2** carrots, chopped
- **2** tomatoes, chopped
- **3** cups cauliflower florets
- **1** can (6 ounces) tomato paste
- **¾** cup water
- **2** teaspoons whole cumin seed
- **½** teaspoon salt
- **½** teaspoon garlic powder
- **1** package (10 ounces) frozen peas, thawed

1. Combine potatoes, onion, bell pepper, carrots and tomatoes in **CROCK-POT**® slow cooker. Stir in cauliflower, tomato paste, water, cumin, salt and garlic powder.

2. Cover; cook on LOW 8 to 9 hours. Stir in peas just before serving.

Makes 6 servings

Nutrition Information:
Serving Size 1½ cups
Calories 191
Total Fat 1g
Saturated Fat 0g
Protein 7g
Carbohydrate 41g
Cholesterol 0mg
Dietary Fiber 9g
Sodium 464mg

Pesto Rice and Beans

1 **can (about 15 ounces) no-salt added Great Northern beans, rinsed and drained**

1 **can (about 14 ounces) fat-free reduced-sodium vegetable broth**

¾ **cup uncooked converted long grain rice**

1½ **cups frozen cut green beans, thawed and drained**

½ **cup prepared pesto**

   Grated Parmesan cheese (optional)

1. Combine Great Northern beans, broth and rice in **CROCK-POT®** slow cooker. Cover; cook on LOW 2 hours.

2. Stir in green beans. Cover; cook on LOW 1 hour or until rice and beans are tender.

3. Turn off heat. Stir in pesto and cheese, if desired. Let stand, covered, 5 minutes or until cheese is melted.

Makes 8 servings

Nutrition Information:
Serving Size ½ cup
Calories 195
Total Fat 8g
Saturated Fat 2g
Protein 7g
Carbohydrate 24g
Cholesterol 5mg
Dietary Fiber 5g
Sodium 245mg

Mushroom and Vegetable Ragoût over Polenta

Ragoût

- **3 tablespoons extra virgin olive oil**
- **8 ounces sliced mushrooms**
- **8 ounces shiitake mushrooms, stemmed and thinly sliced**
- **½ cup Madeira wine**
- **4 cloves garlic, minced**
- **1 medium onion, chopped**
- **1 can (about 15 ounces) reduced-sodium chickpeas, rinsed and drained**
- **1 can (about 28 ounces) crushed tomatoes**
- **1 can (about 6 ounces) tomato paste**
- **1 sprig fresh rosemary, plus additional for garnish**

Polenta

- **2 cups water**
- **2 cups reduced-fat (2%) milk**
- **¼ teaspoon salt**
- **2 cups instant polenta**
- **½ cup grated Parmesan cheese**

1. For ragoût, heat oil in large skillet over medium-high heat. Add mushrooms; cook and stir 8 to 10 minutes or until mushrooms are browned. Add wine; cook 1 minute or until liquid is reduced by one half. Remove to **CROCK-POT®** slow cooker.

2. Stir in garlic, onion, chickpeas, crushed tomatoes, tomato paste and 1 sprig rosemary. Cover; cook on LOW 6 hours. Remove and discard rosemary.

3. For polenta, combine water, milk and salt in large saucepan over medium-high heat. Bring to a boil. Whisk in polenta in slow, steady stream. Cook and whisk 4 to 5 minutes or until thick and creamy. Remove polenta from heat. Stir in cheese; top with ragoût. Garnish with additional rosemary.

Makes 8 servings

Nutrition Information:
Serving Size 1 cup ragoût over ½ cup polenta, **Calories** 340, **Total Fat** 9g, **Saturated Fat** 3g, **Protein** 14g, **Carbohydrate** 51g, **Cholesterol** 10mg, **Dietary Fiber** 9g, **Sodium** 360mg

Italian Eggplant with Millet and Pepper Stuffing ⓁⒻ ⒽⒻ ⓁⓈ Ⓥ

- ¼ cup uncooked millet
- 2 small eggplants (about ¾ pound total), unpeeled
- ¼ cup chopped red bell pepper, divided
- ¼ cup chopped green bell pepper, divided
- 1 teaspoon olive oil
- 1 clove garlic, minced
- 1½ cups fat-free reduced-sodium vegetable broth
- ½ teaspoon ground cumin
- ½ teaspoon dried oregano
- ⅛ teaspoon red pepper flakes

1. Heat large skillet over medium heat. Add millet; cook and stir 5 minutes. Remove to small bowl; set aside. Cut eggplants lengthwise into halves. Scoop out flesh, leaving about ¼-inch-thick shell. Reserve shells; chop eggplant flesh. Combine 1 tablespoon red bell pepper and 1 tablespoon green bell pepper in small bowl; set aside.

2. Heat oil in same skillet over medium heat. Add chopped eggplant, remaining red and green bell peppers and garlic; cook and stir 8 minutes or until eggplant is tender.

3. Combine eggplant mixture, broth, cumin, oregano and red pepper flakes in **CROCK-POT**® slow cooker. Cover; cook on LOW 4½ hours or until all liquid is absorbed.

4. Turn **CROCK-POT**® slow cooker to HIGH. Fill eggplant shells with eggplant-millet mixture. Sprinkle with reserved bell peppers. Place filled shells in **CROCK-POT**® slow cooker. Cover; cook on HIGH 1½ to 2 hours.

Makes 4 servings

Nutrition Information:
Serving Size ½ eggplant with ½ cup stuffing, **Calories** 122, **Total Fat** 3g, **Saturated Fat** 1g, **Protein** 6g, **Carbohydrate** 20g, **Cholesterol** 9mg, **Dietary Fiber** 7g, **Sodium** 99mg

Spinach and Ricotta Stuffed Shells

18 uncooked jumbo pasta shells (about half of a 12-ounce package)

 1 package (15 ounces) reduced-fat ricotta cheese

 7 ounces frozen chopped spinach, thawed and squeezed dry

½ cup grated reduced-fat Parmesan cheese

 1 egg, lightly beaten

 1 clove garlic, minced

½ teaspoon salt

 1 jar (26 ounces) marinara sauce

½ cup (2 ounces) shredded reduced-fat mozzarella cheese

 1 teaspoon olive oil

1. Cook pasta shells according to package directions until almost tender. Drain well. Combine ricotta cheese, spinach, Parmesan cheese, egg, garlic and salt in medium bowl.

2. Pour ¼ cup marinara sauce in bottom of **CROCK-POT**® slow cooker. Spoon 2 to 3 tablespoons ricotta mixture into 1 pasta shell and place in bottom of **CROCK-POT**® slow cooker. Repeat with enough additional shells to cover bottom of **CROCK-POT**® slow cooker. Top with another ¼ cup marinara sauce. Repeat with remaining pasta shells, ricotta mixture and marinara sauce. Top with mozzarella cheese. Drizzle with oil. Cover; cook on HIGH 3 to 4 hours or until mozzarella cheese is melted and sauce is heated through.

Makes 6 servings

Nutrition Information:
Serving Size 3 shells, **Calories** 385, **Total Fat** 8g, **Saturated Fat** 4g, **Protein** 18g, **Carbohydrate** 59g, **Cholesterol** 50mg, **Dietary Fiber** 5g, **Sodium** 727mg

Cornbread and Bean Casserole

Nonstick cooking spray

1 medium yellow onion, chopped

1 medium green bell pepper, chopped

2 cloves garlic, minced

1 can (about 15 ounces) no-salt-added red kidney beans, rinsed and drained

1 can (about 15 ounces) no-salt-added pinto beans, rinsed and drained

1 can (about 14 ounces) no-salt-added diced tomatoes

1 can (8 ounces) no-salt-added tomato sauce

1 teaspoon chili powder

½ teaspoon ground cumin

½ teaspoon black pepper

¼ teaspoon hot pepper sauce

1 cup yellow cornmeal

1 cup all-purpose flour

1 tablespoon sugar

2½ teaspoons baking powder

½ teaspoon salt

1¼ cups reduced-fat (2%) milk

1 can (8½ ounces) cream-style corn

2 eggs

3 tablespoons vegetable oil

1. Coat inside of **CROCK-POT**® slow cooker with nonstick cooking spray. Spray medium skillet with cooking spray; heat over medium heat. Add onion, bell pepper and garlic; cook and stir 3 to 5 minutes or until vegetables are tender. Remove to **CROCK-POT**® slow cooker.

2. Stir in beans, tomatoes, tomato sauce, chili powder, cumin, black pepper and hot pepper sauce. Cover; cook on HIGH 1 hour.

3. Meanwhile, combine cornmeal, flour, sugar, baking powder and salt in large bowl. Combine milk, corn, eggs and oil in small bowl. Add milk mixture to cornmeal mixture; stir just until combined. Spoon evenly over bean mixture in **CROCK-POT**® slow cooker. Cover; cook on HIGH 1½ to 2 hours or until cornbread topping is golden brown.

Makes 8 servings

 Nutrition Information:
Serving Size about 1½ cups, **Calories** 356, **Total Fat** 8g, **Saturated Fat** 1g, **Protein** 14g, **Carbohydrate** 58g, **Cholesterol** 57mg, **Dietary Fiber** 10g, **Sodium** 660mg

No-Fuss Macaroni and Cheese Ⓥ

- **2 cups (about 8 ounces) uncooked elbow macaroni**
- **3 ounces light pasteurized processed cheese product, cubed**
- **1 cup (4 ounces) shredded reduced-fat mild Cheddar cheese**
- **½ teaspoon salt**
- **⅛ teaspoon black pepper**
- **1½ cups fat-free (skim) milk**

Combine macaroni, cheese product, cheese, salt and pepper in **CROCK-POT®** slow cooker. Pour milk over top. Cover; cook on LOW 2 to 3 hours, stirring halfway through cooking time.

Makes 8 servings

Nutrition Information:
Serving Size about ½ cup
Calories 190
Total Fat 5g
Saturated Fat 3g
Protein 11g
Carbohydrate 25g
Cholesterol 15mg
Dietary Fiber 1g
Sodium 470mg

Manchego Eggplant 🅗🅕 🅥

- **1 cup all-purpose flour**
- **4 large eggplants, peeled and sliced horizontally into ¾-inch-thick slices**
- **2 tablespoons olive oil**
- **1 jar (25½ ounces) roasted garlic pasta sauce**
- **2 tablespoons Italian seasoning**
- **1 cup grated manchego cheese**
- **1 jar (24 ounces) roasted eggplant marinara sauce**

1. Place flour in medium shallow bowl. Add eggplant; toss to coat. Heat oil in large skillet over medium-high heat. Lightly brown eggplant in batches 3 to 4 minutes on each side.

2. Pour thin layer of pasta sauce in bottom of **CROCK-POT**® slow cooker. Top with eggplant slices, Italian seasoning, cheese and marinara sauce. Repeat layers until all ingredients have been used. Cover; cook on HIGH 2 hours.

Makes 12 servings

Nutrition Information:
Serving Size 2 slices eggplant with about 1 cup sauce
Calories 204
Total Fat 9g
Saturated Fat 3g
Protein 7g
Carbohydrate 26g
Cholesterol 7mg
Dietary Fiber 6g
Sodium 583mg

Ratatouille with Chickpeas

- **3** tablespoons olive oil, divided
- **4** cloves garlic, minced
- **1** yellow onion, chopped
- **4** small Italian eggplants, peeled and chopped
  Salt and black pepper (optional)
- **1** red bell pepper, chopped
- **1** yellow bell pepper, chopped
- **1** orange bell pepper, chopped
- **3** small zucchini, chopped
- **1** can (about 15 ounces) chickpeas, rinsed and drained
- **2** cups canned crushed tomatoes
- **¼** cup chopped fresh basil
- **2** tablespoons chopped fresh thyme
- **½** to 1 teaspoon red pepper flakes
  Sprigs fresh basil (optional)

1. Heat 1 tablespoon oil in large skillet over medium heat. Add garlic and onion; cook 2 to 3 minutes or until softened. Add eggplants, salt and black pepper, if desired; cook and stir 3 to 5 minutes. Remove to **CROCK-POT®** slow cooker.

2. Add bell peppers, zucchini, chickpeas, tomatoes, chopped basil, thyme, remaining 2 tablespoons oil and red pepper flakes to **CROCK-POT®** slow cooker; stir to blend. Cover; cook on LOW 7 to 8 hours or on HIGH 4½ to 5 hours. Garnish with basil sprigs.

Makes 6 servings

Nutrition Information:
Serving Size about 2 cups, **Calories** 261, **Total Fat** 8g, **Saturated Fat** 1g, **Protein** 9g, **Carbohydrate** 42g, **Cholesterol** 0mg, **Dietary Fiber** 14g, **Sodium** 320mg

Southwestern Corn and Beans

1 **tablespoon olive oil**

1 **large onion, chopped**

1 **jalapeño pepper, diced***

1 **clove garlic, minced**

2 **cans (about 15 ounces *each*) no-salt-added light red kidney beans, rinsed and drained**

1 **bag (16 ounces) frozen corn**

1 **can (about 14 ounces) no-salt-added diced tomatoes**

1 **green bell pepper, cut into 1-inch pieces**

2 **teaspoons chili powder**

½ **teaspoon salt**

½ **teaspoon ground cumin**

½ **teaspoon black pepper**

   Reduced-fat sour cream, sliced black olives and tortilla chips (optional)

Jalapeño peppers can sting and irritate the skin, so wear rubber gloves when handling peppers and do not touch your eyes.

TIP

For a party, spoon this colorful vegetarian dish into hollowed-out bell peppers or bread bowls.

1. Heat oil in large skillet over medium heat. Add onion, jalapeño pepper and garlic; cook and stir 5 minutes. Combine onion mixture, beans, corn, tomatoes, bell pepper, chili powder, salt, cumin and black pepper in **CROCK-POT®** slow cooker; stir to blend.

2. Cover; cook on LOW 7 to 8 hours or on HIGH 2 to 3 hours. Serve with sour cream, olives and tortilla chips, if desired.

Makes 6 servings

 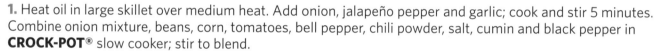

Nutrition Information:

Serving Size about 1 cup, **Calories** 230, **Total Fat** 3g, **Saturated Fat** 1g, **Protein** 12g, **Carbohydrate** 40g, **Cholesterol** 0mg, **Dietary Fiber** 15g, **Sodium** 276mg

Southwestern Stuffed Peppers

- **4** green bell peppers
- **1** can (about 15 ounces) black beans, rinsed and drained
- **1** cup (4 ounces) shredded pepper jack cheese
- **¾** cup medium salsa
- **½** cup frozen corn
- **½** cup chopped green onions
- **⅓** cup uncooked long grain rice
- **1** teaspoon chili powder
- **½** teaspoon ground cumin
  Sour cream (optional)

TIP

For firmer rice, substitute converted rice for regular long grain rice.

1. Cut thin slice off top of each bell pepper. Carefully remove seeds and membranes, leaving peppers whole.

2. Combine beans, cheese, salsa, corn, green onions, rice, chili powder and cumin in medium bowl. Spoon filling evenly into each pepper. Place peppers in **CROCK-POT®** slow cooker. Cover; cook on LOW 4 to 6 hours. Serve with sour cream, if desired.

Makes 4 servings

Nutrition Information:
Serving Size 1 stuffed pepper
Calories 323
Total Fat 10g
Saturated Fat 3g
Protein 15g
Carbohydrate 43g
Cholesterol 30mg
Dietary Fiber 7g
Sodium 796mg

Ziti Ratatouille

2 cans (about 14 ounces *each*) diced tomatoes with garlic and onions

1 jar (about 24 ounces) marinara sauce

1 large eggplant, cut into ½-inch pieces (about 1½ pounds)

2 medium zucchini, cut into ½-inch pieces

1 green or red bell pepper, cut into ½-inch pieces

1 large onion, chopped

4 cloves garlic, minced

1 can (6 ounces) pitted black olives, drained

1 package (8 ounces) uncooked ziti noodles

Lemon juice and grated Parmesan cheese (optional)

1. Combine tomatoes, marinara sauce, eggplant, zucchini, bell pepper, onion and garlic in **CROCK-POT**® slow cooker; stir to blend. Cover; cook on LOW 4½ hours.

2. Stir in olives and pasta. Cover; cook on LOW 25 minutes. Drizzle with lemon juice and sprinkle with cheese, if desired.

Makes 8 servings

Nutrition Information:
Serving Size 1½ cups
Calories 275
Total Fat 7g
Saturated Fat 1g
Protein 8g
Carbohydrate 47g
Cholesterol 2mg
Dietary Fiber 7g
Sodium 692mg

Vegetable-Bean Pasta Sauce

  2 cans (about 15 ounces *each*) cannellini beans, rinsed and drained

  2 cans (about 14 ounces *each*) no-salt-added diced tomatoes

 16 baby carrots

  1 medium onion, sliced

  1 can (6 ounces) tomato paste

  1 ounce dried oyster mushrooms, chopped

 ¼ cup grated Parmesan cheese

  2 teaspoons garlic powder

  1 teaspoon dried basil

  1 teaspoon dried oregano

 ½ teaspoon dried rosemary

 ½ teaspoon dried marjoram

 ½ teaspoon dried sage

 ½ teaspoon dried thyme

 ¼ teaspoon black pepper

  1 package (12 ounces) whole wheat spaghetti noodles, cooked and drained

1. Combine beans, diced tomatoes, carrots, onion, tomato paste, mushrooms, cheese, garlic powder, basil, oregano, rosemary, marjoram, sage, thyme and pepper in **CROCK-POT®** slow cooker; stir to blend.

2. Cover; cook on LOW 8 to 10 hours. Serve over noodles.

Makes 8 servings

Nutrition Information:
Serving Size 1⅓ cups sauce with ¼ cup noodles, **Calories** 310, **Total Fat** 3g, **Saturated Fat** 1g, **Protein** 15g, **Carbohydrate** 60g, **Cholesterol** 0mg, **Dietary Fiber** 13g, **Sodium** 330mg

SOUPS, STEWS AND CHILIES

Caribbean Sweet Potato and Bean Stew 🅷🅕 🆅

- 2 medium sweet potatoes (about 1 pound), cut into 1-inch cubes
- 2 cups frozen cut green beans
- 1 can (about 15 ounces) black beans, rinsed and drained
- 1 can (about 14 ounces) reduced-sodium vegetable broth
- 1 small onion, sliced
- 2 teaspoons Caribbean jerk seasoning
- ½ teaspoon dried thyme
- ¼ teaspoon salt
- ¼ teaspoon ground cinnamon
- ⅓ cup slivered almonds, toasted*

To toast almonds, spread in single layer in heavy skillet. Cook and stir over medium heat 1 to 2 minutes or until nuts are lightly browned.

Combine sweet potatoes, beans, broth, onion, jerk seasoning, thyme, salt and cinnamon in **CROCK-POT**® slow cooker. Cover; cook on LOW 5 to 6 hours. Sprinkle each serving evenly with almonds.

Makes 4 servings

Nutrition Information:
Serving Size about ½ cup, **Calories** 221, **Total Fat** 5g, **Saturated Fat** 0g, **Protein** 9g, **Carbohydrate** 34g, **Cholesterol** 0mg, **Dietary Fiber** 9g, **Sodium** 708mg

Simple Beef Chili HF GF

3 pounds 90% lean ground beef

2 cans (about 14 ounces *each*) unsalted diced tomatoes

2 cans (about 15 ounces *each*) kidney beans, rinsed and drained

2 cups chopped onions

1 package (10 ounces) frozen corn

1 cup chopped green bell pepper

1 can (8 ounces) tomato sauce

3 tablespoons chili powder

1 teaspoon garlic powder

½ teaspoon ground cumin

½ teaspoon dried oregano

Prepared cornbread (optional)

1. Brown beef in large skillet over medium-high heat 6 to 8 minutes, stirring to break up meat. Remove to **CROCK-POT**® slow cooker using slotted spoon.

2. Add tomatoes, beans, onions, corn, bell pepper, tomato sauce, chili powder, garlic powder, cumin and oregano to **CROCK-POT**® slow cooker. Cover; cook on LOW 4 hours. Serve with cornbread, if desired.

Makes 8 servings

Nutrition Information:
Serving Size about ¾ cup, **Calories** 380, **Total Fat** 8g, **Saturated Fat** 3g, **Protein** 42g, **Carbohydrate** 34g, **Cholesterol** 90mg, **Dietary Fiber** 9g, **Sodium** 460mg

Hearty Lentil Stew HF V

1 cup dried lentils, rinsed and sorted

1 package (16 ounces) frozen green beans

2 cups cauliflower florets

1 cup chopped onion

1 cup baby carrots, cut into halves crosswise

3 cups fat-free reduced-sodium vegetable broth

2 teaspoons ground cumin

¾ teaspoon ground ginger

1 can (15 ounces) chunky tomato sauce with garlic and herbs

½ cup dry-roasted peanuts

1. Layer lentils, green beans, cauliflower, onion and carrots in **CROCK-POT®** slow cooker. Combine broth, cumin and ginger in large bowl; stir to blend. Pour over vegetables in **CROCK-POT®** slow cooker.

2. Cover; cook on LOW 9 to 11 hours. Stir in tomato sauce. Cover; cook on LOW 10 minutes or until heated through. Sprinkle each serving evenly with peanuts.

Makes 6 servings

Nutrition Information:
Serving Size 1 cup
Calories 265
Total Fat 7g
Saturated Fat 1g
Protein 15g
Carbohydrate 39g
Cholesterol 0mg
Dietary Fiber 15g
Sodium 504mg

Vegetable Soup with Beans 🅛🅕 🅗🅕 🅥

- **4** cups reduced-sodium vegetable broth
- **1** can (about 15 ounces) cannellini beans, rinsed and drained
- **1** can (about 14 ounces) no-salt-added diced tomatoes
- **16** baby carrots
- **1** medium onion, chopped
- **1** ounce dried oyster mushrooms, chopped
- **3** tablespoons no-salt-added tomato paste
- **2** teaspoons garlic powder
- **1** teaspoon *each* dried basil and dried oregano
- **½** teaspoon *each* dried rosemary, dried marjoram, dried sage and dried thyme
- **¼** teaspoon black pepper
- French bread slices, toasted (optional)

Combine broth, beans, tomatoes, carrots, onion, mushrooms, tomato paste, garlic powder, basil, oregano, rosemary, marjoram, sage, thyme and pepper in **CROCK-POT®** slow cooker. Cover; cook on LOW 8 hours or on HIGH 4 to 5 hours. Serve with bread, if desired.

Makes 4 servings

Nutrition Information:
Serving Size 1 cup
Calories 190
Total Fat 0g
Saturated Fat 0g
Protein 10g
Carbohydrate 37g
Cholesterol 0mg
Dietary Fiber 11g
Sodium 480mg

Pumpkin Soup with Crumbled Bacon and Toasted Pumpkin Seeds 🄷🄵

- 2 **teaspoons olive oil**
- ½ **cup raw pumpkin seeds***
- 2 **slices thick-cut bacon**
- 1 **medium onion, chopped**
- 1 **teaspoon kosher salt**
- ½ **teaspoon chipotle chili powder**
- ½ **teaspoon black pepper**
- 2 **cans (29 ounces *each*) 100% pumpkin purée**
- 4 **cups fat-free reduced-sodium chicken broth**
- ¾ **cup apple cider**
- ½ **cup fat-free half-and-half**
  Sour cream (optional)

Raw pumpkin seeds or pepitas may be found in the produce or ethnic food section of your local supermarket.

1. Coat inside of **CROCK-POT®** slow cooker with nonstick cooking spray. Heat oil in small skillet over medium-high heat. Add pumpkin seeds; stir until seeds begin to pop, about 1 minute. Spoon into small bowl; set aside.

2. Add bacon to skillet; cook and stir until crisp. Remove bacon to paper-towel lined plate using slotted spoon. Reserve drippings in skillet. Crumble bacon when cool enough to handle; set aside. Reduce heat to medium. Add onion to skillet; cook and stir 3 minutes or until translucent. Stir in salt, chili powder and pepper. Remove to **CROCK-POT®** slow cooker.

3. Whisk pumpkin purée, broth and cider into **CROCK-POT®** slow cooker until smooth. Cover; cook on HIGH 4 hours.

4. Turn off heat. Whisk in half-and-half; strain soup evenly into bowls. Garnish with pumpkin seeds, bacon and sour cream, if desired.

Makes 6 servings

Nutrition Information:
Serving Size about 1½ cups, **Calories** 250, **Total Fat** 12g, **Saturated Fat** 2g, **Protein** 11g, **Carbohydrate** 30g, **Cholesterol** 5mg, **Dietary Fiber** 12g, **Sodium** 750mg

Wild Mushroom Beef Stew

1½ to 2 pounds cubed beef stew meat

2 tablespoons all-purpose flour

½ teaspoon salt

½ teaspoon black pepper

1½ cups fat-free reduced-sodium beef broth

1 teaspoon Worcestershire sauce

1 clove garlic, minced

1 whole bay leaf

1 teaspoon paprika

4 shiitake mushrooms, sliced

2 medium carrots, sliced

2 medium potatoes, chopped

1 small onion, chopped

1 medium stalk celery, sliced

TIP

This classic beef stew is given a twist with the addition of flavorful shiitake mushrooms. If shiitake mushrooms are unavailable in your local grocery store, you can substitute other mushrooms of your choice. For extra punch, add a few dried porcini mushrooms to the stew.

1. Place beef in **CROCK-POT**® slow cooker. Combine flour, salt and pepper in small bowl; stir to blend. Place flour mixture in **CROCK-POT**® slow cooker; toss to coat meat. Add broth, Worcestershire sauce, garlic, bay leaf, paprika, mushrooms, carrots, potatoes, onion and celery.

2. Cover; cook on LOW 10 to 12 hours or on HIGH 4 to 6 hours. Remove and discard bay leaf. Stir to blend before serving.

Makes 8 servings

Note: You may double the amount of meat, mushrooms, carrots, potatoes, onion and celery for a 5-, 6- or 7-quart **CROCK-POT**® slow cooker.

Nutrition Information:
Serving Size about ¾ cup, **Calories** 210, **Total Fat** 9g, **Saturated Fat** 3g, **Protein** 19g, **Carbohydrate** 13g, **Cholesterol** 55mg, **Dietary Fiber** 2g, **Sodium** 320mg

Chipotle Vegetable Chili with Chocolate HF V

2 tablespoons olive oil

1 medium onion, chopped

1 medium green bell pepper, chopped

1 medium red bell pepper, chopped

1 cup frozen corn

1 can (28 ounces) no-salt-added diced tomatoes

1 can (about 15 ounces) reduced-sodium black beans, rinsed and drained

1 can (about 15 ounces) reduced-sodium pinto beans, rinsed and drained

1 tablespoon chili powder

1 teaspoon ground cumin

½ teaspoon chipotle chili powder

1 ounce semisweet chocolate, chopped

1. Heat oil in large skillet over medium-high heat. Add onion and bell peppers; cook and stir 4 minutes or until softened. Stir in corn; cook 3 minutes. Remove to **CROCK-POT**® slow cooker.

2. Stir tomatoes, beans, chili powder, cumin and chipotle chili powder into **CROCK-POT**® slow cooker. Cover; cook on LOW 6 to 7 hours. Stir chocolate into **CROCK-POT**® slow cooker until melted.

Makes 6 servings

Nutrition Information:
Serving Size 1 cup
Calories 230
Total Fat 6g
Saturated Fat 2g
Protein 9g
Carbohydrate 38g
Cholesterol 0mg
Dietary Fiber 11g
Sodium 240mg

Savory Bean Stew 🄻🄵 🄷🄵 🅅

- 1 can (about 15 ounces) no-salt-added chickpeas, rinsed and drained
- 1 can (about 15 ounces) reduced-sodium pinto beans, rinsed and drained
- 1 can (about 15 ounces) reduced-sodium black beans, rinsed and drained
- 1 can (about 14 ounces) no-salt-added diced tomatoes
- 1 cup frozen vegetable blend (onions, celery, red and green bell peppers)
- ¾ teaspoon dried thyme
- ¾ teaspoon dried sage
- ½ to ¾ teaspoon dried oregano
- ¾ cup vegetable broth, divided
- 1 tablespoon all-purpose flour
- Prepared polenta (optional)

1. Combine chickpeas, beans, tomatoes, vegetable blend, thyme, sage and oregano in **CROCK-POT®** slow cooker. Stir ½ cup broth into flour in small bowl until smooth. Whisk flour mixture into bean mixture. Cover; cook on LOW 4 hours.

2. Stir remaining ¼ cup broth into **CROCK-POT®** slow cooker. Serve with polenta, if desired.

Makes 6 servings

Nutrition Information:
Serving Size about ½ cup
Calories 200
Total Fat 1g
Saturated Fat 0g
Protein 11g
Carbohydrate 38g
Cholesterol 0mg
Dietary Fiber 12g
Sodium 300mg

Garlic Lentil Soup with Mushrooms and Greens

- ¾ cup olive oil
- 1 whole head garlic
- 2 tablespoons fresh rosemary
- 3 medium stalks celery, diced
- 2 medium onions, chopped
- 1 bag (16 ounces) green lentils
- 12 fresh sage leaves
- 12 cups reduced-sodium vegetable broth
- 1 package (8 ounces) mushrooms
- 8 ounces kale, spinach or Swiss chard, coarsely chopped
- 6 tablespoons grated reduced-fat Parmesan or Romano cheese (optional)

  Chopped fresh Italian parsley (optional)

1. Place oil, garlic, and rosemary in small heatproof bowl; cover with foil. Place bowl in **CROCK-POT**® slow cooker. Cover; cook on HIGH 1½ hours. Drain, reserving garlic oil and garlic cloves separately; refrigerate. Discard rosemary. (This portion of the recipe can be prepared up to 2 days in advance.)

2. Heat 2 tablespoons garlic oil in large skillet over medium-high heat. Add celery and onions; cook and stir until onions caramelize. Remove to **CROCK-POT**® slow cooker. Add lentils, sage, broth and mushrooms. Cover; cook on LOW 8 hours or on HIGH 4 hours.

3. Heat 3 to 4 tablespoons garlic oil in skillet over medium heat. Add kale; cook and stir just until tender. Stir kale into soup. Sprinkle with cheese and parsley, if desired.

Makes 10 servings

Nutrition Information:
Serving Size 2 cups, **Calories** 280, **Total Fat** 5g, **Saturated Fat** 1g, **Protein** 15g, **Carbohydrate** 47g, **Cholesterol** 0mg, **Dietary Fiber** 13g, **Sodium** 250mg

Curried Vegetable and Cashew Stew HF V

1 medium potato, cut into ½-inch cubes

1 can (about 15 ounces) no-salt-added chickpeas, rinsed and drained

1 can (about 14 ounces) no-salt-added diced tomatoes

1 medium (about ½ pound) eggplant, cut into ½-inch cubes

1 medium onion, chopped

1 cup reduced-sodium vegetable broth

2 tablespoons quick-cooking tapioca

2 teaspoons grated fresh ginger

2 teaspoons curry powder

½ teaspoon salt

¼ teaspoon black pepper

1 medium zucchini (about 8 ounces), cut into ½-inch cubes

2 tablespoons golden raisins

½ cup frozen peas

½ cup lightly salted cashews

1. Combine potato, chickpeas, tomatoes, eggplant, onion, broth, tapioca, ginger, curry powder, salt and pepper in **CROCK-POT®** slow cooker. Cover; cook on LOW 8 to 9 hours.

2. Stir zucchini, raisins, peas and cashews into **CROCK-POT®** slow cooker. Turn **CROCK-POT®** slow cooker to HIGH. Cover; cook on HIGH 1 hour or until zucchini is tender.

Makes 8 servings

Nutrition Information:
Serving Size 1 cup, **Calories** 220, **Total Fat** 8g, **Saturated Fat** 2g, **Protein** 8g, **Carbohydrate** 31g, **Cholesterol** 0mg, **Dietary Fiber** 6g, **Sodium** 230mg

Kick'n Chili GF

2 **pounds (32 ounces) 95% lean ground beef**

1 **tablespoon ground cumin**

1 **tablespoon dried oregano**

1 **tablespoon chili powder**

1 **tablespoon paprika**

1 **tablespoon black pepper**

2 **cloves garlic, minced**

2 **teaspoons red pepper flakes**

1½ **teaspoons salt**

¼ **teaspoon ground red pepper**

1 **tablespoon vegetable oil**

3 **cans (10½ ounces *each*) diced tomatoes with mild green chiles**

1 **jar (16 ounces) salsa**

1 **medium onion, chopped**

1. Combine beef, cumin, oregano, chili powder, paprika, black pepper, garlic, red pepper flakes, salt and ground red pepper in large bowl. Heat oil in large skillet over medium-high heat. Add beef mixture; cook and stir 6 to 8 minutes or until browned. Remove beef mixture to **CROCK-POT®** slow cooker using slotted spoon.

2. Add tomatoes, salsa and onion; stir to blend. Cover; cook on LOW 4 to 6 hours.

Makes 8 servings

Note: Reduce red pepper flakes for a milder flavor.

Nutrition Information:
Serving Size about ¾ cup, **Calories** 230, **Total Fat** 8g, **Saturated Fat** 3g, **Protein** 26g, **Carbohydrate** 12g, **Cholesterol** 70mg, **Dietary Fiber** 3g, **Sodium** 790mg

Classic Beef Stew

2½ pounds cubed beef stew meat

¼ cup all-purpose flour

2 tablespoons olive oil

3 cups fat-free reduced-sodium beef broth

16 baby carrots

8 fingerling potatoes, halved crosswise

1 medium onion, chopped

1 ounce dried oyster mushrooms, chopped

2 teaspoons garlic powder

1 teaspoon dried basil

1 teaspoon dried oregano

½ teaspoon dried rosemary

½ teaspoon dried marjoram

½ teaspoon dried sage

½ teaspoon dried thyme

Salt and black pepper (optional)

Fresh chopped Italian parsley (optional)

1. Combine beef and flour in large bowl; toss well to coat. Heat 1 tablespoon oil in large skillet over medium-high heat. Add half of beef; cook and stir 4 minutes or until browned. Remove to 6-quart **CROCK-POT**® slow cooker. Repeat with remaining oil and beef.

2. Add broth, carrots, potatoes, onion, mushrooms, garlic powder, basil, oregano, rosemary, marjoram, sage and thyme to **CROCK-POT**® slow cooker; stir to blend. Cover; cook on LOW 10 to 12 hours or on HIGH 5 to 6 hours. Season with salt and pepper, if desired. Garnish with parsley.

Makes 8 servings

Nutrition Information:
Serving Size about ½ cup, **Calories** 440, **Total Fat** 15g, **Saturated Fat** 5g, **Protein** 52g, **Carbohydrate** 25g, **Cholesterol** 140mg, **Dietary Fiber** 2g, **Sodium** 480mg

Roasted Tomato-Basil Soup 🅛🄵 🅥

2 cans (28 ounces *each*) whole tomatoes, drained and 3 cups juice reserved

2½ tablespoons packed dark brown sugar

1 medium onion, finely chopped

3 cups fat-free reduced-sodium vegetable broth

3 tablespoons tomato paste

¼ teaspoon ground allspice

1 can (5 ounces) evaporated milk

¼ cup chopped fresh basil

Salt and black pepper (optional)

Fresh basil leaves (optional)

1. Preheat oven to 450°F. Line baking sheet with foil; spray with nonstick cooking spray. Arrange tomatoes on foil in single layer. Top with brown sugar and onion. Bake 25 minutes or until tomatoes look dry and light brown. Let tomatoes cool slightly; finely chop.

2. Combine tomato mixture, 3 cups reserved juice, broth, tomato paste and allspice in **CROCK-POT**® slow cooker; stir to blend. Cover; cook on LOW 8 hours or on HIGH 4 hours.

3. Add evaporated milk and ¼ cup chopped basil; season with salt and pepper, if desired. Cover; cook on HIGH 30 minutes or until heated through. Garnish with basil leaves.

Makes 8 servings

Nutrition Information:
Serving Size about 1 cup
Calories 100
Total Fat 2g
Saturated Fat 1g
Protein 4g
Carbohydrate 17g
Cholesterol 5mg
Dietary Fiber 2g
Sodium 620mg

Three-Bean Chipotle Chili HF V GF

- 2 tablespoons olive oil
- 1 large onion, chopped
- 1 medium green bell pepper, chopped
- 2 cloves garlic, minced
- 2 cans (about 15 ounces *each*) pinto beans, rinsed and drained
- 1 can (about 15 ounces) small white beans, rinsed and drained
- 1 can (about 15 ounces) chickpeas, rinsed and drained
- 1 cup water
- 1 cup frozen corn
- 1 can (6 ounces) tomato paste
- 1 or 2 canned chipotle chiles in adobo sauce, finely chopped

Optional toppings: sour cream, shredded Cheddar cheese and/or chopped onion

1. Heat oil in large skillet over medium heat. Add onion, bell pepper and garlic; cook and stir 5 minutes or until onion is softened. Remove to **CROCK-POT**® slow cooker.

2. Stir in beans, chickpeas, water, corn, tomato paste and chipotle chiles. Cover; cook on LOW 3½ to 4 hours. Top as desired.

Makes 8 servings

Nutrition Information:
Serving Size about ½ cup
Calories 220
Total Fat 5g
Saturated Fat 1g
Protein 10g
Carbohydrate 35g
Cholesterol 0mg
Dietary Fiber 9g
Sodium 790mg

Pasta Fagioli Soup HF V

2 cans (about 14 ounces *each*) fat-free reduced-sodium vegetable broth

1 can (about 15 ounces) Great Northern beans, rinsed and drained

1 can (about 14 ounces) diced tomatoes

2 medium zucchini, quartered lengthwise and sliced

1 tablespoon olive oil

1½ teaspoons minced garlic

½ teaspoon dried basil

½ teaspoon dried oregano

½ cup uncooked ditalini, tubetti or small shell pasta

½ cup garlic seasoned croutons

½ cup grated Asiago or Romano cheese

3 tablespoons chopped fresh basil or Italian parsley (optional)

TIP

Only small pasta varieties like ditalini or tubetti pasta should be used in this recipe. The low heat of a CROCK-POT® slow cooker will not allow larger pasta shapes to cook completely.

1. Combine broth, beans, tomatoes, zucchini, oil, garlic, dried basil and oregano in **CROCK-POT®** slow cooker; stir to blend. Cover; cook on LOW 3 to 4 hours.

2. Stir in pasta. Cover; cook on LOW 1 hour or until pasta is tender. Serve with croutons and cheese. Garnish with fresh basil.

Makes 6 servings

Nutrition Information:
Serving Size 1¾ cups, **Calories** 200, **Total Fat** 7g, **Saturated Fat** 3g, **Protein** 11g, **Carbohydrate** 24g, **Cholesterol** 10mg, **Dietary Fiber** 6g, **Sodium** 750mg

Chicken Tortilla Soup 🅷🅵

- **1 pound boneless, skinless chicken breasts**
- **2 cans (15 ounces *each*) diced tomatoes**
- **1 can (4 ounces) chopped mild green chiles, drained**
- **½ cup fat-free chicken broth**
- **1 medium yellow onion, chopped**
- **2 cloves garlic, minced**
- **1 teaspoon ground cumin**
- **Salt and black pepper (optional)**
- **4 corn tortillas, sliced into ¼-inch strips**
- **2 tablespoons chopped fresh cilantro**
- **½ cup (2 ounces) shredded Monterey Jack cheese**
- **1 avocado, diced and tossed with lime juice**

1. Place chicken in **CROCK-POT**® slow cooker. Combine tomatoes, chiles, broth, onion, garlic and cumin in medium bowl; pour over chicken. Cover; cook on LOW 6 hours or on HIGH 3 hours.

2. Remove chicken to cutting board. Shred with two forks; return to cooking liquid. Season with salt and pepper, if desired.

3. Just before serving, add tortillas and cilantro to **CROCK-POT**® slow cooker; stir to blend. Top each serving evenly with cheese and avocado.

Makes 6 servings

Nutrition Information:
Serving Size about 1¼ cups
Calories 254
Total Fat 10g
Saturated Fat 3g
Protein 22g
Carbohydrate 19g
Cholesterol 57mg
Dietary Fiber 5g
Sodium 573mg

Black and White Chili HF GF

Nonstick cooking spray

1 **pound boneless, skinless chicken breasts, cut into ¾-inch pieces**

1 **cup chopped onion**

1 **can (about 15 ounces) Great Northern beans, rinsed and drained**

1 **can (about 15 ounces) reduced-sodium black beans, rinsed and drained**

1 **can (about 14 ounces) reduced-sodium stewed tomatoes, undrained**

2 **tablespoons Texas-style chili seasoning mix**

TIP

For a change of pace, this delicious chili is excellent served over cooked rice.

1. Spray large skillet with cooking spray; heat over medium heat. Add chicken and onion; cook and stir 5 minutes or until chicken is browned.

2. Combine chicken mixture, beans, tomatoes and chili seasoning in **CROCK-POT**® slow cooker. Cover; cook on LOW 4 to 4½ hours.

Makes 6 servings

Nutrition Information:

Serving Size 1 cup
Calories 353
Total Fat 12g
Saturated Fat 3g
Protein 20g
Carbohydrate 43g
Cholesterol 31mg
Dietary Fiber 9g
Sodium 681mg

Vegetarian Chili   GF

- **1 tablespoon vegetable oil**
- **1 cup chopped onion**
- **1 cup chopped red bell pepper**
- **2 tablespoons minced jalapeño pepper***
- **1 clove garlic, minced**
- **1 can (about 28 ounces) reduced-sodium stewed tomatoes**
- **1 can (about 15 ounces) black beans, rinsed and drained**
- **1 can (about 15 ounces) chickpeas, rinsed and drained**
- **½ cup frozen corn**
- **¼ cup tomato paste**
- **1 teaspoon sugar**
- **1 teaspoon ground cumin**
- **1 teaspoon dried basil**
- **1 teaspoon chili powder**
- **¼ teaspoon black pepper**
- **Sour cream and shredded Cheddar cheese (optional)**

Jalapeño peppers can sting and irritate the skin, so wear rubber gloves when handling peppers and do not touch your eyes.

1. Heat oil in large skillet over medium-high heat. Add onion, bell pepper, jalapeño pepper and garlic; cook and stir 5 minutes. Remove onion mixture to **CROCK-POT**® slow cooker using slotted spoon. Add tomatoes, beans, chickpeas, corn, tomato paste, sugar, cumin, basil, chili powder and black pepper; stir to blend.

2. Cover; cook on LOW 4 to 5 hours. Serve with sour cream and cheese, if desired.

Makes 4 servings

Nutrition Information:
Serving Size 1¼ cups, **Calories** 329, **Total Fat** 6g, **Saturated Fat** 0g, **Protein** 15g, **Carbohydrate** 57g, **Cholesterol** 0mg, **Dietary Fiber** 14g, **Sodium** 858mg

Summary Vegetable Stew ⓛⓕ ⓗⓕ ⓥ

- **1** cup reduced-sodium vegetable broth
- **1** can (about 15 ounces) chickpeas, rinsed and drained
- **1** medium zucchini, cut into ½-inch pieces
- **1** summer squash, cut into ½-inch pieces
- **4** large plum tomatoes, cut into ½-inch pieces
- **1** cup frozen corn
- **½** to 1 teaspoon dried rosemary
- **¼** cup grated Asiago or Parmesan cheese
- **1** tablespoon chopped fresh Italian parsley

Combine broth, chickpeas, zucchini, squash, tomatoes, corn and rosemary in **CROCK-POT**® slow cooker; stir to blend. Cover; cook on LOW 8 hours or on HIGH 5 hours. Top each serving evenly with cheese and parsley.

Makes 4 servings

Nutrition Information:
Serving Size 1 cup
Calories 168
Total Fat 3g
Saturated Fat 7g
Protein 9g
Carbohydrate 28g
Cholesterol 3mg
Dietary Fiber 6g
Sodium 317mg

Sweet Red Bell Pepper Soup 🄛🅂 🅅 🄶🄵

- **2 tablespoons olive oil**
- **8 red bell peppers, sliced into quarters**
- **1 onion, thinly sliced**
- **3 cloves garlic, minced**
- **1 teaspoon black pepper**
- **1 teaspoon dried oregano**
- **2 tablespoons balsamic vinegar**
- **2 teaspoons sugar**
- **Sprigs fresh thyme (optional)**

1. Coat inside of **CROCK-POT**® slow cooker with oil. Add bell peppers, onion, garlic, black pepper and oregano; stir to blend. Cover; cook on HIGH 4 hours or until bell peppers are very tender, stirring halfway through cooking time.

2. Remove soup in batches to blender or food processor; blend until smooth. Return soup to **CROCK-POT**® slow cooker. Stir in balsamic vinegar and sugar. Ladle soup into bowls; garnish with thyme sprigs.

Makes 8 servings

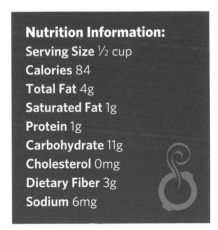

Nutrition Information:
Serving Size ½ cup
Calories 84
Total Fat 4g
Saturated Fat 1g
Protein 1g
Carbohydrate 11g
Cholesterol 0mg
Dietary Fiber 3g
Sodium 6mg

Braised Pork Shanks with Israeli Couscous and Root Vegetable Stew 🅷🅵

   4 **pork shanks, bone in, skin removed (about 1½ pounds total)**
      Coarse salt and black pepper (optional)
   2 **tablespoons olive oil**
   4 **large carrots, sliced diagonally into 1-inch pieces and divided**
   4 **stalks celery, sliced diagonally into 1-inch pieces and divided**
   1 **large yellow onion, quartered**
   4 **cloves garlic, crushed**
   4 **cups fat-free reduced-sodium chicken broth**
   2 **cups dry white wine**
   ¼ **cup no-salt-added tomato paste**
   ¼ **cup distilled white vinegar**
   2 **tablespoons mustard oil (optional)***
   1 **tablespoon whole black peppercorns**
      Israeli Couscous (recipe follows)

Mustard oil is available at Middle Eastern specialty shops or in the supermarket ethnic foods aisle.

1. Season pork with salt and black pepper, if desired. Heat oil in large skillet over medium heat. Add pork; cook 5 to 7 minutes or until browned on all sides. Remove to **CROCK-POT**® slow cooker.

2. Pour off all but 2 tablespoons oil in skillet. Add half of carrots, half of celery, onion and garlic; cook and stir 5 minutes or until vegetables are soft but not brown. Remove to **CROCK-POT**® slow cooker.

3. Add broth, wine, tomato paste, vinegar, mustard oil, if desired, and peppercorns to skillet; cook and stir 5 to 7 minutes, scraping up any browned bits from skillet. Pour over shanks in **CROCK-POT**® slow cooker. Cover; cook on HIGH 2 hours, turning pork every 20 minutes.

4. Strain cooking liquid; discard solids. Return cooking liquid to **CROCK-POT**® slow cooker. Add remaining half of carrots and celery. Cover; cook on HIGH 1 hour. Remove pork to large plate; cover loosely with foil to keep warm.

5. Meanwhile, prepare Israeli Couscous.

6. Add Israeli Couscous to **CROCK-POT**® slow cooker. Cover; cook on HIGH 5 to 10 minutes or until heated through. Place couscous and vegetables in shallow bowls; top each with 1 pork shank. Spoon ¼ cup cooking liquid into each bowl.

Makes 4 servings

Israeli Couscous

2 **cups water**

Pinch salt

1⅓ **cups Israeli or regular couscous**

Place water and salt in large saucepan over medium-low heat; bring to a boil over high heat. Add couscous; cook and stir 6 to 8 minutes or until tender. Rinse and drain under cold water.

Makes about 2 cups

Nutrition Information:
Serving Size 1 pork shank with 1 cup stew, **Calories** 459, **Total Fat** 12g, **Saturated Fat** 3g, **Protein** 31g, **Carbohydrate** 44g, **Cholesterol** 68mg, **Dietary Fiber** 5g, **Sodium** 488mg

Chili Verde

Nonstick cooking spray

¾ **pound boneless lean pork, cut into 1-inch cubes**

1 **pound fresh tomatillos, husks removed, rinsed and coarsely chopped**

1 **can (about 15 ounces) Great Northern beans, rinsed and drained**

1 **can (about 14 ounces) fat-free reduced-sodium chicken broth**

1 **large onion, halved and thinly sliced**

1 **can (4 ounces) diced mild green chiles**

6 **cloves garlic, sliced**

1 **teaspoon ground cumin**

Salt and black pepper (optional)

½ **cup lightly packed fresh cilantro, chopped**

1. Spray large skillet with cooking spray; heat over medium-high heat. Add pork; cook and stir 5 to 7 minutes or until browned on all sides.

2. Combine pork, tomatillos, beans, broth, onion, chiles, garlic and cumin in **CROCK-POT**® slow cooker. Cover; cook on HIGH 3 to 4 hours.

3. Season with salt and pepper, if desired. Turn **CROCK-POT**® slow cooker to LOW. Stir in cilantro. Cover; cook on LOW 10 minutes.

Makes 4 servings

 Nutrition Information:
Serving Size 2½ cups, **Calories** 250, **Total Fat** 4g, **Saturated Fat** 1g, **Protein** 26g, **Carbohydrate** 28g, **Cholesterol** 55mg, **Dietary Fiber** 10g, **Sodium** 680mg

Chili with Turkey and Beans LF HF

2 cans (about 14 ounces *each*) no-salt-added whole tomatoes, drained

2 cans (about 15 ounces *each*) no-salt-added red kidney beans, rinsed and drained

1 pound cooked 99% fat-free ground turkey

1 can (about 15 ounces) reduced-sodium black beans, rinsed and drained

1 can (12 ounces) no-salt-added tomato sauce

1 cup finely chopped yellow onion

1 cup finely chopped celery

1 cup finely chopped carrot

½ cup amaretto (optional)

3 tablespoons chili powder

1 tablespoon Worcestershire sauce

1 tablespoon plus 1 teaspoon ground cumin

2 teaspoons ground red pepper

1 teaspoon salt

Shredded Cheddar cheese (optional)

Combine tomatoes, kidney beans, turkey, black beans, tomato sauce, onion, celery, carrot, amaretto, if desired, chili powder, Worcestershire sauce, cumin, ground red pepper and salt in **CROCK-POT**® slow cooker. Cover; cook on HIGH 7 hours. Sprinkle with cheese, if desired.

Makes 6 servings

Nutrition Information:
Serving Size about 1¼ cups
Calories 301
Total Fat 2g
Saturated Fat 0g
Protein 33g
Carbohydrate 43g
Cholesterol 30mg
Dietary Fiber 18g
Sodium 771mg

Parsnip and Carrot Soup LF HF V

Nonstick cooking spray

1 medium leek, thinly sliced

4 medium parsnips, chopped

4 medium carrots, chopped

4 cups fat-free reduced-sodium vegetable broth

1 whole bay leaf

¼ teaspoon salt

½ teaspoon black pepper

2 ounces small pasta, cooked and drained

1 tablespoon chopped fresh Italian parsley

1 cup fat-free croutons (optional)

1. Spray small skillet with cooking spray; heat over medium heat. Add leek; cook 3 to 5 minutes or until golden. Remove to **CROCK-POT**® slow cooker.

2. Add parsnips, carrots, broth, bay leaf, salt and pepper. Cover; cook on LOW 6 to 9 hours or on HIGH 2 to 4 hours. Add pasta during last hour of cooking.

3. Remove and discard bay leaf. Sprinkle each serving evenly with parsley and croutons, if desired.

Makes 4 servings

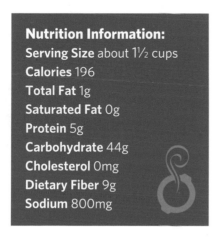

Nutrition Information:
Serving Size about 1½ cups
Calories 196
Total Fat 1g
Saturated Fat 0g
Protein 5g
Carbohydrate 44g
Cholesterol 0mg
Dietary Fiber 9g
Sodium 800mg

PORK-PACKED FAVORITES

Andouille and Cabbage Crock

Nonstick cooking spray

1 pound andouille sausage, cut into 3- to 4-inch pieces

1 small head cabbage, cut into 8 wedges

1 medium onion, cut into ½-inch wedges

3 medium carrots, quartered lengthwise
and cut into 3-inch pieces

8 new potatoes, cut in half

½ cup apple juice

1 can (about 14 ounces) fat-free reduced-sodium chicken broth

Honey mustard (optional)

Crusty rolls (optional)

Andouille is a spicy, smoked pork sausage. Feel free to substitute your favorite smoked sausage or kielbasa.

1. Coat inside of **CROCK-POT**® slow cooker with cooking spray. Spray large skillet with cooking spray; heat over medium-high heat. Add sausage; cook and stir 6 to 8 minutes or until browned. Remove from heat.

2. Add cabbage, onion, carrots, potatoes, apple juice and broth to **CROCK-POT**® slow cooker; top with sausage. Cover; cook on HIGH 4 hours or until cabbage is tender. Remove with slotted spoon to large serving bowl. Serve with honey mustard and crusty rolls, if desired.

Makes 8 servings

Nutrition Information:
Serving Size 1 piece sausage, 1 wedge cabbage, 2 potato halves and 3 pieces carrot, **Calories** 200, **Total Fat** 8g, **Saturated Fat** 3g, **Protein** 12g, **Carbohydrate** 19g, **Cholesterol** 35mg, **Dietary Fiber** 4g, **Sodium** 560mg

Spicy Asian Pork Bundles

1 **lean boneless pork sirloin roast (about 3 pounds)***

½ **cup reduced-sodium soy sauce**

1 **tablespoon chili paste or chili garlic sauce**

2 **teaspoons minced fresh ginger**

2 **tablespoons water**

1 **tablespoon cornstarch**

2 **teaspoons dark sesame oil**

1 **cup shredded carrots**

10 **large romaine lettuce leaves**

Unless you have a 5-, 6- or 7-quart **CROCK-POT® slow cooker, cut any roast larger than 2½ pounds in half so il cooks completely.*

1. Combine pork, soy sauce, chili paste and ginger in **CROCK-POT**® slow cooker; stir to blend. Cover; cook on LOW 8 to 10 hours.

2. Turn off heat. Remove roast from cooking liquid; cool slightly. Trim and discard excess fat. Shred pork with two forks. Let cooking liquid stand 5 minutes to allow fat to rise. Skim off and discard fat.

3. Turn **CROCK-POT**® slow cooker to HIGH. Stir water, cornstarch and sesame oil in small bowl until smooth; whisk into cooking liquid. Cook, uncovered, on HIGH 15 minutes or until thickened.

4. Return pork to **CROCK-POT**® slow cooker; stir in carrots. Cover; cook on HIGH 15 to 30 minutes or until heated through. Spoon ½ cup pork onto each lettuce leaf. Wrap to enclose.

Makes 10 servings

Mu Shu Pork Bundles: Lightly spread prepared plum sauce over small warm flour tortillas. Spoon ¼ cup pork filling and ¼ cup stir-fried vegetables into flour tortillas. Wrap to enclose. Makes 10 servings.

Nutrition Information:
Serving Size 1 bundle, **Calories** 240, **Total Fat** 5g, **Saturated Fat** 1g, **Protein** 44g, **Carbohydrate** 4g, **Cholesterol** 115mg, **Dietary Fiber** 1g, **Sodium** 610mg

Spicy Citrus Pork with Pineapple Salsa

- 1 **tablespoon ground cumin**
- 1 **teaspoon black pepper**
- ½ **teaspoon salt**
- 3 **pounds boneless lean center-cut pork loin, rinsed and patted dry**
- 2 **tablespoons vegetable oil**
- 4 **cans (8 ounces** *each***) pineapple tidbits in own juice, drained and ½ cup juice reserved***
- 3 **tablespoons lemon juice, divided**
- 1 **cup finely chopped orange or red bell pepper**
- ¼ **cup finely chopped red onion**
- 2 **tablespoons chopped fresh cilantro or mint**
- 2 **teaspoons grated lemon peel**
- 1 **teaspoon grated fresh ginger (optional)**
- ¼ **teaspoon red pepper flakes (optional)**

If tidbits are unavailable, purchase pineapple chunks and coarsely chop.

1. Coat inside of **CROCK-POT**® slow cooker with nonstick cooking spray. Combine cumin, black pepper and salt in small bowl. Rub evenly onto pork. Heat oil in medium skillet over medium-high heat. Brown pork on all sides, 1 to 2 minutes per side. Remove to **CROCK-POT**® slow cooker.

2. Spoon 4 tablespoons of reserved pineapple juice and 2 tablespoons lemon juice over pork. Cover; cook on LOW 2 to 2¼ hours or on HIGH 1 hour and 10 minutes or until meat is tender.

3. Meanwhile, combine pineapple, remaining 4 tablespoons pineapple juice, remaining 1 tablespoon lemon juice, bell pepper, onion, cilantro, lemon peel, ginger, if desired, and red pepper flakes, if desired, in medium bowl. Toss gently; set aside.

4. Remove pork to large serving platter. Let pork stand 10 minutes before slicing into six pieces. Arrange pork slices on serving platter. To serve, pour sauce evenly over slices. Serve with salsa.

Makes 6 servings

Nutrition Information:
Serving Size 1 slice pork with about ½ cup salsa, **Calories** 210, **Total Fat** 6g, **Saturated Fat** 2g, **Protein** 26g, **Carbohydrate** 12g, **Cholesterol** 65mg, **Dietary Fiber** 1g, **Sodium** 170mg

Pork Loin Stuffed with Stone Fruits (GF)

1 **boneless pork loin roast (about 4 pounds)***

¾ **teaspoon salt**

½ **teaspoon black pepper**

2 **tablespoons olive oil, divided**

1 **medium yellow onion, chopped**

½ **cup Madeira or dry sherry wine**

½ **cup dried pitted plums**

½ **cup dried peaches**

½ **cup dried apricots**

2 **cloves garlic, minced**

¼ **teaspoon dried thyme**

To butterfly a roast means to split the meat down the center without cutting all the way through. This allows the meat to be spread open so a filling can be added.

*Unless you have a 5-, 6- or 7-quart **CROCK-POT®** slow cooker, cut any roast larger than 2½ pounds in half so it cooks completely.*

1. Coat inside of **CROCK-POT®** slow cooker with nonstick cooking spray. Season pork with salt and pepper. Heat 1 tablespoon oil in large skillet over medium-high heat. Add pork; cook and stir 6 to 8 minutes or until browned on all sides. Remove pork to cutting board, browned side down.

2. Add remaining 1 tablespoon oil to same skillet; heat over medium heat. Add onion; cook and stir 3 to 5 minutes or until tender. Add wine; cook 2 to 3 minutes or until mixture reduces slightly. Stir in dried fruit, garlic and thyme; cook 1 minute. Remove skillet from heat.

3. Butterfly roast lengthwise to within 1½ inches of edge. Spoon fruit mixture onto pork roast; bring sides together to close roast. Slide kitchen string under roast and tie roast shut, allowing 2 inches between ties. Place roast in **CROCK-POT®** slow cooker. Cover; cook on LOW 5 to 6 hours or on HIGH 2 to 3 hours.

4. Remove roast to cutting board. Cover loosely with foil; let stand 10 to 15 minutes before slicing into 10 pieces.

Makes 10 servings

Nutrition Information:
Serving Size 1 piece stuffed pork, **Calories** 319, **Total Fat** 11g, **Saturated Fat** 3g, **Protein** 39g, **Carbohydrate** 14g, **Cholesterol** 114mg, **Dietary Fiber** 2g, **Sodium** 270mg

Pork Chops à l'Orange GF

1 tablespoon extra virgin olive oil

8 lean bone-in pork loin chops

⅓ cup orange juice

2 tablespoons clover honey

1 teaspoon salt

1 teaspoon packed brown sugar

1 teaspoon grated orange peel

¼ cup water

2 tablespoons cornstarch

1. Heat oil in large skillet over medium-high heat. Add pork chops in batches; cook 1 to 2 minutes or until browned on both sides.

2. Combine orange juice, honey, salt, brown sugar and orange peel in **CROCK-POT**® slow cooker. Add chops, turning each chop to coat well. Cover; cook on LOW 6 to 8 hours.

3. Remove pork to large plate. Turn **CROCK-POT**® slow cooker to HIGH. Stir water into cornstarch in small bowl until smooth. Whisk cornstarch mixture into orange sauce or until thickened. Spoon sauce evenly over pork to serve.

Makes 8 servings

Nutrition Information:
Serving Size 1 pork chop with about 2 tablespoons sauce, **Calories** 197, **Total Fat** 7g, **Saturated Fat** 2g, **Protein** 23g, **Carbohydrate** 7g, **Cholesterol** 63mg, **Dietary Fiber** 0g, **Sodium** 347mg

Simple Shredded Pork Tacos

1¾ **pounds lean boneless pork roast**

1 **cup salsa**

1 **can (4 ounces) chopped mild green chiles**

½ **teaspoon garlic salt**

½ **teaspoon black pepper**

6 **(8-inch) corn tortillas**

Optional toppings: sour cream, diced tomatoes and/or sliced jalapeño peppers

TIP

Cut the pork roast to fit in the bottom of your CROCK-POT® slow cooker in one or two layers.

1. Place roast, salsa, chiles, garlic salt and pepper in **CROCK-POT®** slow cooker. Cover; cook on LOW 8 hours.

2. Remove pork from **CROCK-POT®** slow cooker; shred with two forks. Spoon shredded pork evenly into tortillas with sauce. Top as desired.

Makes 6 servings

Nutrition Information:
Serving Size 1 taco
Calories 190
Total Fat 4g
Saturated Fat 2g
Protein 30g
Carbohydrate 4g
Cholesterol 75mg
Dietary Fiber 1g
Sodium 370mg

German Kraut and Sausage 🄷🄵 🄶🄵

- 5   medium potatoes, cut into ½-inch pieces
- 1   large yellow onion, cut into ¼-inch slices
- ½   green bell pepper, chopped
- 1   can (16 ounces) sauerkraut
- 1   pound reduced-fat smoked sausage, cut into 1-inch pieces
- ¼   cup packed brown sugar
- 1   teaspoon garlic powder
- ½   teaspoon black pepper

1. Layer potatoes, onion, bell pepper and sauerkraut in **CROCK-POT**® slow cooker. Brown sausage in large skillet over medium-high heat. Remove to **CROCK-POT**® slow cooker using slotted spoon.

2. Combine brown sugar, garlic powder and black pepper in small bowl; stir to combine. Sprinkle evenly over sausage. Cover; cook on LOW 8 hours.

Makes 8 servings

Nutrition Information:
Serving Size about 1¼ cups
Calories 282
Total Fat 11g
Saturated Fat 4g
Protein 13g
Carbohydrate 34g
Cholesterol 41mg
Dietary Fiber 5g
Sodium 550mg

Pork Meatballs in Garlicky Almond Sauce

½ cup blanched whole almonds

1 cup fat-free reduced-sodium chicken broth

⅓ cup roasted red pepper

4 teaspoons minced garlic, divided

1 teaspoon salt, divided

½ teaspoon crushed saffron threads (optional)

1 cup fresh bread crumbs, divided

¼ cup dry white wine

1 pound extra lean ground pork

¼ cup finely chopped onion

1 egg, lightly beaten

3 tablespoons minced fresh Italian parsley

Nonstick cooking spray

1. Place almonds in food processor or blender; pulse until finely ground. Add broth, red pepper, 2 teaspoons garlic, ½ teaspoon salt and saffron, if desired; process until smooth. Stir in ¼ cup bread crumbs. Remove to **CROCK-POT®** slow cooker.

2. Place remaining ¾ cup bread crumbs in large bowl; sprinkle with wine. Add pork, onion, egg, parsley, remaining 2 teaspoons garlic and ½ teaspoon salt; stir to blend. Shape pork mixture into 24 meatballs.

3. Spray large skillet with cooking spray; heat over medium-high heat. Add meatballs in batches; cook and stir 5 to 7 minutes or until browned on all sides. Remove to **CROCK-POT®** slow cooker. Cover; cook on HIGH 3 to 4 hours.

Makes 6 servings

Nutrition Information:
Serving Size 4 meatballs, **Calories** 230, **Total Fat** 11g, **Saturated Fat** 2g, **Protein** 21g, **Carbohydrate** 11g, **Cholesterol** 80mg, **Dietary Fiber** 2g, **Sodium** 720mg

Cajun-Style Country Ribs GF

2 cups baby carrots

1 medium onion, coarsely chopped

1 green bell pepper, cut into 1-inch pieces

1 red bell pepper, cut into 1-inch pieces

2 teaspoons minced garlic

2 tablespoons Creole seasoning, divided

3 pounds country-style pork ribs, trimmed and cut evenly into 8 portions

1 can (about 14 ounces) no-salt-added stewed tomatoes, undrained

2 tablespoons water

1 tablespoon cornstarch

Hot cooked rice (optional)

1. Combine carrots, onion, bell peppers, garlic and 2 teaspoons seasoning in **CROCK-POT**® slow cooker; stir to blend.

2. Sprinkle ribs with 1 tablespoon seasoning; place in **CROCK-POT**® slow cooker. Pour tomatoes over ribs. Cover; cook on LOW 6 to 8 hours.

3. Remove ribs and vegetables from **CROCK-POT**® slow cooker using slotted spoon. Turn off heat. Let liquid stand 15 minutes; skim off fat.

4. Turn **CROCK-POT**® slow cooker to HIGH. Stir water into cornstarch and remaining 1 teaspoon seasoning in small bowl until smooth. Whisk into **CROCK-POT**® slow cooker. Cook, uncovered, on HIGH 15 minutes or until thickened. Return ribs and vegetables to sauce; carefully stir to coat. Serve over rice, if desired.

Makes 8 servings

Nutrition Information:
Serving Size 1 portion ribs with about ½ cup vegetables, **Calories** 286, **Total Fat** 10g, **Saturated Fat** 2g, **Protein** 36g, **Carbohydrate** 10g, **Cholesterol** 126mg, **Dietary Fiber** 2g, **Sodium** 587mg

Simply Delicious Pork Roast GF

1½ pounds boneless pork loin, cut into 6 pieces or 6 boneless pork loin chops

4 medium Golden Delicious apples, cored and sliced

3 tablespoons packed light brown sugar

1 teaspoon ground cinnamon

½ teaspoon salt

1. Place pork in **CROCK-POT**® slow cooker; cover with apples.

2. Combine brown sugar, cinnamon and salt in small bowl; sprinkle over apples. Cover; cook on LOW 6 to 8 hours.

Makes 6 servings

Nutrition Information:
Serving Size 1 slice pork with about 1 cup apples with sauce
Calories 222
Total Fat 4g
Saturated Fat 1g
Protein 26g
Carbohydrate 21g
Cholesterol 65mg
Dietary Fiber 2g
Sodium 259mg

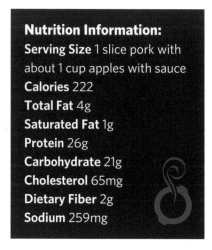

Rough-Cut Smoky Red Pork Roast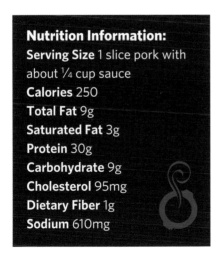

1 can (about 14 ounces) stewed tomatoes, drained

1 can (6 ounces) tomato paste with basil, oregano and garlic

1 cup chopped red bell pepper

2 to 3 canned chipotle peppers in adobo sauce, finely chopped and mashed with fork*

1 teaspoon salt

1 lean pork shoulder roast (about 3¼ pounds)**

1½ to 2 tablespoons sugar

For less heat, remove seeds from chipotle peppers before mashing.

Unless you have a 5-, 6- or 7-quart **CROCK-POT® slow cooker, cut any roast larger than 2½ pounds in half so it cooks completely.*

1. Coat inside of **CROCK-POT**® slow cooker with nonstick cooking spray.

2. Combine stewed tomatoes, tomato paste, bell pepper, chipotle peppers and salt in **CROCK-POT**® slow cooker. Add pork, fat side up. Cover; cook on HIGH 5 hours.

3. Remove pork to cutting board. Cover loosely with foil; let stand 10 to 15 minutes. Stir sugar into cooking liquid. Cook, uncovered, on HIGH 15 minutes. To serve, remove fat from pork and slice into ten pieces. Pour sauce evenly over pork slices.

Makes 10 servings

Nutrition Information:
Serving Size 1 slice pork with about ¼ cup sauce
Calories 250
Total Fat 9g
Saturated Fat 3g
Protein 30g
Carbohydrate 9g
Cholesterol 95mg
Dietary Fiber 1g
Sodium 610mg

Pork Roast with Fruit Medley GF

1 **boneless pork loin roast (about 4 pounds)***

1 **tablespoon black pepper**

2 **teaspoons salt**

   Nonstick cooking spray

2 **cups green grapes**

1 **cup dried apricots**

1 **cup dried prunes**

2 **whole bay leaves**

1 **teaspoon dried thyme**

2 **cloves garlic, minced**

1 **cup dry red wine**

   Juice of ½ lemon

*Unless you have a 5-, 6- or 7-quart **CROCK-POT®** slow cooker, cut any roast larger than 2½ pounds in half so it cooks completely.*

1. Season pork with pepper and salt. Spray large skillet with cooking spray; heat over medium-high heat. Add pork; cook 5 to 7 minutes or until browned on all sides.

2. Combine grapes, apricots, prunes, bay leaves, thyme, garlic, wine and lemon juice in **CROCK-POT®** slow cooker; stir to blend. Add pork to **CROCK-POT®** slow cooker; turn to coat. Cover; cook on LOW 7 to 9 hours or on HIGH 3 to 5 hours. Remove and discard bay leaves. Remove roast to cutting board. Cut roast evenly into eight pieces.

Makes 8 servings

Nutrition Information:
Serving Size 1 piece pork with about 1½ cups sauce, **Calories** 441, **Total Fat** 10g, **Saturated Fat** 3g, **Protein** 49g, **Carbohydrate** 32g, **Cholesterol** 142mg, **Dietary Fiber** 3g, **Sodium** 776mg

Vegetable-Stuffed Pork Chops

4 lean bone-in pork chops

Salt and black pepper

1 cup frozen corn

1 medium green bell pepper, chopped

½ cup Italian-style seasoned dry bread crumbs

1 small onion, chopped

½ cup uncooked converted long grain rice

1 can (8 ounces) tomato sauce

Your butcher can cut a pocket in the pork chops to save you time and to ensure even cooking.

1. Cut pocket into each pork chop, cutting from edge to bone. Lightly season pockets with salt and pepper. Combine corn, bell pepper, bread crumbs, onion and rice in large bowl; stir to blend. Stuff pork chops with rice mixture. Secure open side with toothpicks.

2. Place any remaining rice mixture in **CROCK-POT**® slow cooker. Add stuffed pork chops to **CROCK-POT**® slow cooker. Pour tomato sauce over pork chops. Cover; cook on LOW 8 to 10 hours.

3. Remove pork chops to large serving platter. Remove and discard toothpicks. Serve with extra rice mixture.

Makes 4 servings

Nutrition Information:
Serving Size 1 pork chop with 1 cup stuffing, **Calories** 330, **Total Fat** 7g, **Saturated Fat** 2g, **Protein** 25g, **Carbohydrate** 40g, **Cholesterol** 50mg, **Dietary Fiber** 4g, **Sodium** 720mg

Pork Roast Landaise ⒽⒻ

2½ pounds boneless center-cut pork loin roast
     Salt and black pepper (optional)

2 tablespoons olive oil

1 medium yellow onion, diced

2 cloves garlic, minced

2 teaspoons dried thyme

2 parsnips, cut into ¾-inch slices

¼ cup red wine vinegar

¼ cup sugar

2 cups fat-free reduced-sodium chicken broth, divided

2 tablespoons cornstarch

3 pears, cored and sliced ¾ inch thick

1 cup pitted prunes

1. Season pork with salt and pepper, if desired. Heat oil in large skillet over medium-high heat. Add pork; cook 5 to 7 minutes on each side until browned. Remove to **CROCK-POT**® slow cooker using slotted spoon.

2. Add onion and garlic to skillet; cook and stir 2 to 3 minutes. Stir in thyme. Remove to **CROCK-POT**® slow cooker. Add parsnips; stir well.

3. Combine vinegar and sugar in same skillet; cook and stir 5 to 7 minutes or until thickened. Add 1¾ cups broth. Stir remaining ¼ cup of broth into cornstarch in small bowl until smooth. Whisk cornstarch mixture into skillet; cook until slightly thickened. Pour into **CROCK-POT**® slow cooker.

4. Cover; cook on LOW 8 hours or on HIGH 4 hours. Add pears and prunes during last 30 minutes of cooking. Remove roast to cutting board. Cut roast evenly into eight pieces.

Makes 8 servings

Nutrition Information:
Serving Size 1 pork slice with ½ cup pear and prune mixture with sauce, **Calories** 400, **Total Fat** 9g, **Saturated Fat** 3g, **Protein** 34g, **Carbohydrate** 45g, **Cholesterol** 95mg, **Dietary Fiber** 6g, **Sodium** 190mg

Lemon Pork Chops

1 tablespoon vegetable oil

4 lean boneless pork loin chops

3 cans (8 ounces *each*) no-salt-added tomato sauce

1 large yellow onion, quartered and sliced

1 large green bell pepper, cut into strips

1 tablespoon lemon-pepper seasoning

1 tablespoon Worcestershire sauce

1 large lemon, quartered, plus additional for garnish

TIP

Browning pork before adding it to the CROCK-POT® slow cooker helps reduce the fat. Just remember to drain off the fat in the skillet before removing the pork to the CROCK-POT® slow cooker.

1. Heat oil in large skillet over medium-low heat. Add pork chops; cook 3 to 5 minutes or until browned on both sides. Drain fat. Remove pork to **CROCK-POT®** slow cooker.

2. Combine tomato sauce, onion, bell pepper, lemon-pepper seasoning and Worcestershire sauce in medium bowl. Add to **CROCK-POT®** slow cooker.

3. Squeeze juice from 4 lemon quarters over sauce mixture; drop squeezed lemons into **CROCK-POT®** slow cooker. Cover; cook on LOW 6 to 8 hours or until pork is tender. Remove squeezed lemons before serving. Garnish with additional fresh lemon quarters.

Makes 4 servings

Nutrition Information:
Serving Size 1 pork chop with ½ cup sauce, **Calories** 279, **Total Fat** 10g, **Saturated Fat** 2g, **Protein** 26g, **Carbohydrate** 21g, **Cholesterol** 63mg, **Dietary Fiber** 4g, **Sodium** 332mg

# HEARTY BEEF DINNERS

Brisket with Sweet Onions

- **2 large sweet onions, cut into 10 (½-inch) slices***
- **1 flat-cut boneless beef brisket (about 3½ pounds)**
  Salt and black pepper (optional)
- **2 cans (about 14 ounces *each*)**
  fat-free reduced-sodium beef broth
- **1 teaspoon cracked black peppercorns**
- **3 ounces crumbled bleu cheese (optional)**

*Preferably Maui, Vidalia or Walla Walla onions.

TIP

Use freshly ground pepper as a quick and simple flavor enhancer for CROCK-POT® slow cooker dishes.

1. Coat inside of **CROCK-POT®** slow cooker with nonstick cooking spray. Line bottom with onion slices.

2. Season brisket with salt and pepper, if desired. Heat large skillet over medium-high heat. Add brisket; cook 10 to 12 minutes or until browned on all sides. Remove to **CROCK-POT®** slow cooker.

3. Pour broth into **CROCK-POT®** slow cooker. Sprinkle brisket with peppercorns. Cover; cook on HIGH 5 to 7 hours.

4. Remove brisket to cutting board. Cover loosely with foil; let stand 10 to 15 minutes. Slice against the grain into ten slices. To serve, arrange onions on serving platter and spread slices of brisket on top. Sprinkle with blue cheese, if desired. Serve with cooking liquid.

Makes 10 servings

Nutrition Information:
Serving Size 1 slice beef and 1 slice onion with about ¼ cup cooking liquid, **Calories** 410, **Total Fat** 22g, **Saturated Fat** 8g, **Protein** 46g, **Carbohydrate** 5g, **Cholesterol** 145mg, **Dietary Fiber** 1g, **Sodium** 280mg

Delicious Pepper Steak

2 tablespoons toasted sesame oil

2 pounds beef round steak, cut into strips

½ medium red bell pepper, sliced

½ medium green bell pepper, sliced

½ medium yellow bell pepper, sliced

1 medium onion, sliced

14 grape tomatoes

⅓ cup hoisin sauce

¼ cup water

3 tablespoons all-purpose flour

3 tablespoons reduced-sodium soy sauce

2 teaspoons garlic powder

1 teaspoon ground cumin

1 teaspoon dried oregano

1 teaspoon paprika

⅛ teaspoon ground red pepper

Hot cooked rice (optional)

1. Heat oil in large skillet over medium-high heat. Add beef in batches; cook 4 to 5 minutes or until browned. Remove to large paper towel-lined plate.

2. Add bell peppers, onion and tomatoes to **CROCK-POT**® slow cooker. Combine hoisin sauce, water, flour, soy sauce, garlic powder, cumin, oregano, paprika and ground red pepper in medium bowl; stir to blend. Add to **CROCK-POT**® slow cooker. Top with beef. Cover; cook on LOW 8 to 9 hours or on HIGH 4 to 4½ hours. Serve with rice, if desired.

Makes 6 servings

Nutrition Information:
Serving Size 1 cup, **Calories** 450, **Total Fat** 19g, **Saturated Fat** 6g, **Protein** 53g, **Carbohydrate** 15g, **Cholesterol** 145mg, **Dietary Fiber** 2g, **Sodium** 590mg

Asian Ginger Beef over Bok Choy

- 2 tablespoons peanut oil
- 1½ pounds boneless beef chuck roast, cut into 1-inch pieces
- 3 green onions, cut into ½-inch slices
- 6 cloves garlic
- 1 cup fat-free reduced-sodium chicken broth
- ½ cup water
- ¼ cup reduced-sodium soy sauce
- 2 teaspoons ground ginger
- 1 teaspoon Asian chili paste
- 9 ounces fresh udon noodles or vermicelli, cooked and drained
- 9 ounces bok choy, trimmed, washed and cut into 1-inch pieces
- ½ cup minced fresh cilantro (optional)

1. Heat oil in large skillet over medium-high heat. Add beef in batches with green onions and garlic; cook and stir 6 to 8 minutes or until beef is browned on all sides. Remove to **CROCK-POT**® slow cooker. Add broth, water, soy sauce, ginger and chili paste; stir to blend. Cover; cook on LOW 7 to 8 hours or on HIGH 3 to 4 hours.

2. Stir in noodles and bok choy. Cover; cook on HIGH 15 minutes or until bok choy is tender-crisp. Garnish with cilantro.

Makes 8 servings

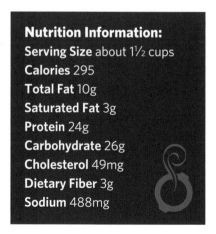

Nutrition Information:
Serving Size about 1½ cups
Calories 295
Total Fat 10g
Saturated Fat 3g
Protein 24g
Carbohydrate 26g
Cholesterol 49mg
Dietary Fiber 3g
Sodium 488mg

Yankee Pot Roast and Vegetables (LS)

3 unpeeled medium baking potatoes (about 1 pound), cut into quarters

2 large carrots, cut into ¾-inch slices

2 stalks celery, cut into ¾-inch slices

1 medium yellow onion, sliced

1 large parsnip, cut into ¾-inch slices

2 whole bay leaves

1 teaspoon dried rosemary

½ teaspoon dried thyme

2½ pounds beef chuck pot roast, cut into 1-inch pieces

Salt and black pepper (optional)

½ cup fat-free reduced-sodium beef broth

1. Combine potatoes, carrots, celery, onion, parsnip, bay leaves, rosemary and thyme in **CROCK-POT®** slow cooker. Season beef with salt and pepper, if desired. Place beef over vegetables. Pour broth over beef.

2. Cover; cook on LOW 8½ to 9 hours. Remove beef to large serving platter; arrange vegetables around beef. Remove and discard bay leaves.

Makes 12 servings

Nutrition Information:
Serving Size about 1¼ cups
Calories 182
Total Fat 4g
Saturated Fat 2g
Protein 22g
Carbohydrate 13g
Cholesterol 42mg
Dietary Fiber 3g
Sodium 110mg

Polenta with Beef Chile Sauce

- 2 **tablespoons vegetable oil**
- 2 **pounds lean beef round roast, cut into 1-inch pieces**
- 1 **medium yellow onion, finely chopped**
- 2 **cloves garlic, diced**
- 1¾ **cups water**
- 5 **canned whole mild green chiles, peeled and diced***
- 1 **canned chipotle pepper in adobo sauce, diced***
- 1 **teaspoon salt**
- 1 **teaspoon all-purpose flour**
- 1 **teaspoon dried oregano**
- ½ **teaspoon ground cumin**
- ¼ **teaspoon black pepper**
  - **Prepared polenta (optional)**
  - **Fresh cilantro (optional)**

Green chiles and chipotle peppers can sting and irritate the skin, so wear rubber gloves when handling peppers and do not touch your eyes.

1. Heat oil in large skillet over medium heat. Add beef; cook 6 to 8 minutes or until browned on all sides. Add onion and garlic during last few minutes of browning. Remove to **CROCK-POT®** slow cooker.

2. Add water, chiles and chipotle pepper; stir to combine. Cover; cook on LOW 2 hours.

3. Combine salt, flour, oregano, cumin and black pepper in small bowl; stir to blend. Add to **CROCK-POT®** slow cooker. Cover; cook on LOW 3 to 4 hours. Serve beef mixture over polenta, if desired. Garnish with cilantro.

Makes 6 servings

Nutrition Information:
Serving Size about 1¼ cups, **Calories** 251, **Total Fat** 11g, **Saturated Fat** 3g, **Protein** 34g, **Carbohydrate** 4g, **Cholesterol** 88mg, **Dietary Fiber** 1g, **Sodium** 527mg

Deep Dark Black Coffee'd Beef

- **2** cups sliced mushrooms
- **1** cup chopped onions
- **2** teaspoons instant coffee granules
- **1½** teaspoons chili powder
- **½** teaspoon black pepper
- **1** lean boneless beef chuck roast (about 2 pounds)
- **1** tablespoon vegetable oil
- **½** cup water
- **1** tablespoon Worcestershire sauce
- **1** teaspoon reduced-sodium beef bouillon granules or 1 bouillon cube
- **½** teaspoon garlic powder
- Hot cooked asparagus (optional)

TIP

"Au jus" means "with juice," and usually refers to the cooking liquid in which meats have cooked. If you prefer a thicker sauce, blend 1 tablespoon cornstarch and 2 tablespoons water. Whisk into the cooking liquid and continue cooking until it thickens.

1. Coat inside of **CROCK-POT**® slow cooker with nonstick cooking spray. Add mushrooms and onions.

2. Combine coffee granules, chili powder and pepper in small bowl; stir to blend. Rub evenly onto beef. Heat oil in large skillet over medium-high heat. Brown beef 3 minutes per side or until browned. Place beef on vegetables in **CROCK-POT**® slow cooker.

3. Add water, Worcestershire sauce, bouillon granules and garlic powder. Cover; cook on LOW 8 hours or HIGH 4 hours.

4. Remove beef to large serving platter. Pour cooking liquid through fine-mesh sieve to drain well, reserving liquid and vegetables. Place vegetables over beef. Allow cooking liquid to stand 2 to 3 minutes. Skim and discard excess fat. Serve with remaining liquid and asparagus, if desired.

Makes 6 servings

Nutrition Information:
Serving Size 1 cup, **Calories** 360, **Total Fat** 14g, **Saturated Fat** 5g, **Protein** 54g, **Carbohydrate** 4g, **Cholesterol** 155mg, **Dietary Fiber** 1g, **Sodium** 190mg

Shredded Beef Wraps

1 lean beef flank steak or beef skirt steak (1 to 1½ pounds), cut into 4 equal pieces

1 cup fat-free reduced-sodium beef broth

½ cup sun-dried tomatoes (not packed in oil), chopped

3 to 4 cloves garlic, minced

¼ teaspoon ground cumin

4 (8-inch) flour tortillas

Optional toppings: shredded lettuce, diced tomatoes and/or shredded Monterey Jack cheese

1. Combine beef, broth, sun-dried tomatoes, garlic and cumin in **CROCK-POT®** slow cooker. Cover; cook on LOW 7 to 8 hours.

2. Remove beef from **CROCK-POT®** slow cooker. Shred with two forks. Place remaining contents from **CROCK-POT®** slow cooker in blender or food processor; blend until smooth.

3. Spoon beef and sauce evenly onto tortillas. Top as desired. Roll up to serve.

Makes 4 servings

Nutrition Information:
Serving Size 1 wrap
Calories 280
Total Fat 9g
Saturated Fat 3g
Protein 28g
Carbohydrate 21g
Cholesterol 35mg
Dietary Fiber 1g
Sodium 540mg

Slow Cooker Meat Loaf

1½ pounds extra lean ground beef

¾ cup fat-free (skim) milk

⅔ cup fine plain dry bread crumbs

2 eggs, beaten

2 tablespoons minced onion

¾ teaspoon salt

½ teaspoon ground sage

½ cup ketchup

2 tablespoons packed brown sugar

1 teaspoon dry mustard

1. Combine beef, milk, bread crumbs, eggs, onion, salt and sage in large bowl; shape into ball. Place in **CROCK-POT**® slow cooker. Cover; cook on LOW 5 to 6 hours.

2. Turn **CROCK-POT**® slow cooker to HIGH. Combine ketchup, brown sugar and mustard in small bowl. Pour over meat loaf in **CROCK-POT**® slow cooker. Cover; cook on HIGH 15 minutes. Cut meat loaf evenly into six slices.

Makes 6 servings

Nutrition Information:
Serving Size 1 slice
Calories 250
Total Fat 7g
Saturated Fat 3g
Protein 27g
Carbohydrate 20g
Cholesterol 130mg
Dietary Fiber 1g
Sodium 710mg

Sirloin Tips with Caramelized Onion Brandy Sauce

  3 **tablespoons all-purpose flour**

  ½ **teaspoon salt**

  ½ **teaspoon crushed whole black peppercorns**

1½ **pounds beef sirloin tips, cut into 2-inch pieces**

  ½ **cup fat-free reduced-sodium beef broth**

  3 **tablespoons brandy**

  1 **teaspoon Worcestershire sauce**

  1 **clove garlic, minced**

  1 **medium sweet onion, thinly sliced and separated into rings**

  1 **tablespoon packed brown sugar**

  ¼ **teaspoon ground red pepper**

  ¼ **cup half-and-half**

    Hot cooked wild rice (optional)

1. Combine flour, salt and peppercorns in large bowl. Add beef; toss to coat. Remove to **CROCK-POT**® slow cooker.

2. Combine broth, brandy, Worcestershire sauce and garlic in small bowl; pour over beef. Combine onion, brown sugar and ground red pepper in small bowl; toss to coat. Remove to **CROCK-POT**® slow cooker. Cover; cook on LOW 6 to 8 hours.

3. Turn **CROCK-POT**® slow cooker to HIGH. Stir in half-and-half. Cover; cook on HIGH 15 minutes. Serve beef and sauce over wild rice, if desired.

Makes 4 servings

Nutrition Information:
Serving Size 1 cup, **Calories** 370, **Total Fat** 13g, **Saturated Fat** 4g, **Protein** 38g, **Carbohydrate** 15g, **Cholesterol** 110mg, **Dietary Fiber** 1g, **Sodium** 480mg

Herbed Pot Roast with Fingerling Potatoes

  1 (3-pound) boneless beef chuck roast

  ¼ cup all-purpose flour

  2 tablespoons olive oil

16 baby carrots

  8 fingerling potatoes, halved crosswise

  1 medium onion, chopped

  2 teaspoons garlic powder

  1 teaspoon dried basil

  1 teaspoon dried oregano

  ½ teaspoon dried rosemary

  ½ teaspoon dried marjoram

  ½ teaspoon dried sage

  ½ teaspoon dried thyme

  ¼ teaspoon black pepper

1½ cups fat-free reduced-sodium beef broth

1. Combine beef and flour in large bowl; toss to coat. Heat oil in large skillet over medium-high heat. Remove beef from flour, reserving flour. Add beef to skillet; cook 6 to 8 minutes or until browned.

2. Meanwhile, add carrots, potatoes, onion, garlic powder, basil, oregano, rosemary, marjoram, sage, thyme and pepper to **CROCK-POT®** slow cooker. Combine reserved flour with broth in small bowl; add to **CROCK-POT®** slow cooker. Top with beef.

3. Cover; cook on LOW 10 to 12 hours or on HIGH 5 to 6 hours. Remove beef to cutting board. Cover loosely with foil; let stand 10 to 15 minutes before evenly slicing into eight pieces. Serve with gravy and vegetables.

Makes 8 servings

Nutrition Information:
Serving Size 1 piece roast with 1 potato, 2 carrots and ¼ cup sauce, **Calories** 460, **Total Fat** 13g, **Saturated Fat** 4g, **Protein** 51g, **Carbohydrate** 32g, **Cholesterol** 140mg, **Dietary Fiber** 3g, **Sodium** 180mg

Thai Steak Salad

Steak

- ¼ cup soy sauce
- 3 cloves garlic, minced
- 3 tablespoons honey
- 1 pound lean boneless beef chuck roast, about ¾ inch thick

Dressing

- ¼ cup hoisin sauce
- 2 tablespoons reduced-fat creamy peanut butter
- ½ cup water
- 1 tablespoon minced fresh ginger
- 1 tablespoon tomato paste or ketchup
- 2 teaspoons lime juice
- 1 teaspoon sugar
- 2 cloves garlic, minced
- ¼ teaspoon hot chili sauce or sriracha*

Salad

- 1½ pounds shredded savoy cabbage
- 1 bag (10 ounces) romaine lettuce with carrots and red cabbage
- 1 cup fresh cilantro leaves
- ½ cup chopped dry-roasted, lightly salted peanuts
- 1 cup chopped mango

  Fresh lime wedges

**Because the CROCK-POT®
slow cooker cooks at a low heat
for a long time, it's perfect for
dishes calling for less-tender
cuts of meat.**

Sriracha is a Thai hot sauce, sometimes called "rooster sauce," because of the label on the bottle. It is available in Asian specialty markets.

1. For steak, coat inside of **CROCK-POT®** slow cooker with nonstick cooking spray. Combine soy sauce, garlic and honey in small bowl. Pour into **CROCK-POT®** slow cooker. Add steak; turn to coat. Cover; cook on HIGH 3 hours or until beef is tender.

2. Remove beef to cutting board. Cover loosely with foil; let stand 10 to 15 minutes before slicing against the grain into ¼-inch strips. Cover; refrigerate until needed.

3. For dressing, blend hoisin sauce and peanut butter in small bowl until smooth. Add water, ginger, tomato paste, lime juice, sugar, 2 cloves garlic and chili sauce; stir to blend.

4. For salad, toss cabbage and romaine salad mixture with dressing in large bowl. Top with reserved steak. Sprinkle with cilantro, peanuts and mango. Serve with lime wedges.

Makes 10 servings

Nutrition Information:
Serving Size 2 ounces steak with about 1 tablespoon dressing on ½ cup salad, **Calories** 240, **Total Fat** 12g, **Saturated Fat** 3g, **Protein** 15g, **Carbohydrate** 20g, **Cholesterol** 25mg, **Dietary Fiber** 3g, **Sodium** 750mg

Russian Borscht

- 4 cups thinly sliced green cabbage
- 1½ pounds fresh beets, shredded
- 5 small carrots, halved lengthwise then cut into 1-inch pieces
- 1 parsnip, peeled, halved lengthwise then cut into 1-inch pieces
- 1 cup chopped onion
- 4 cloves garlic, minced
- 1 pound cubed beef stew meat
- 1 can (about 14 ounces) diced tomatoes
- 3 cans (about 14 ounces *each*) fat-free reduced-sodium beef broth
- ¼ cup lemon juice
- 1 tablespoon sugar
- 1 teaspoon black pepper

  Chopped fresh Italian parsley (optional)

Layer cabbage, beets, carrots, parsnip, onion, garlic, beef, tomatoes, broth, lemon juice, sugar and pepper in **CROCK-POT®** slow cooker. Cover; cook on LOW 7 to 9 hours. Garnish with parsley.

Makes 12 servings

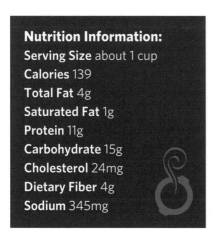

Nutrition Information:
Serving Size about 1 cup
Calories 139
Total Fat 4g
Saturated Fat 1g
Protein 11g
Carbohydrate 15g
Cholesterol 24mg
Dietary Fiber 4g
Sodium 345mg

Ginger Beef with Peppers and Mushrooms

1½ pounds beef top round steak, cut into ¾-inch cubes

24 baby carrots

1 red bell pepper, chopped

1 green bell pepper, chopped

1 medium yellow onion, chopped

1 package (8 ounces) mushrooms, halved

2 tablespoons grated fresh ginger

1 cup fat-free reduced-sodium beef broth

½ cup hoisin sauce

¼ cup quick-cooking tapioca

Hot cooked rice (optional)

Combine beef, carrots, bell peppers, onion, mushrooms, ginger, broth, hoisin sauce and tapioca in **CROCK-POT®** slow cooker; stir to blend. Cover; cook on LOW 8 to 9 hours. Serve over rice, if desired.

Makes 6 servings

Nutrition Information:
Serving Size about 1 cup
Calories 349
Total Fat 11g
Saturated Fat 4g
Protein 38g
Carbohydrate 25g
Cholesterol 66mg
Dietary Fiber 3g
Sodium 502mg

Merlot'd Beef and Sun-Dried Tomato Portobello Ragoût

1 jar (7 ounces) sun-dried tomatoes packed in oil, drained, with 3 tablespoons oil reserved

1 lean boneless beef chuck roast (about 2¾ pounds), cut into 1½-inch pieces

1 can (about 14 ounces) fat-free reduced-sodium beef broth

6 ounces sliced portobello mushrooms

1 medium green bell pepper, cut into thin strips

1 medium orange or yellow bell pepper, cut into thin strips

1 medium onion, cut into 8 wedges

2 teaspoons dried oregano

½ teaspoon salt

¼ teaspoon garlic powder

½ cup Merlot or other dry red wine

2 tablespoons Worcestershire sauce

1 tablespoon balsamic vinegar

1 tablespoon cornstarch

Black pepper

Mashed potatoes, rice or egg noodles (optional)

1. Heat reserved oil in large skillet over medium-high heat. Add beef in batches; cook 6 to 8 minutes or until browned on all sides. Remove to **CROCK-POT**® slow cooker.

2. Add broth to skillet; cook and stir 5 to 7 minutes, scraping up any browned bits from skillet. Pour mixture over beef. Add sun-dried tomatoes, mushrooms, bell peppers, onion, oregano, salt and garlic powder to **CROCK-POT**® slow cooker.

3. Combine wine and Worcestershire sauce in small bowl; reserve ¼ cup. Gently stir remaining wine mixture into **CROCK-POT**® slow cooker. Cover; cook on LOW 8 to 9 hours or on HIGH 4 to 5 hours.

4. Stir vinegar and cornstarch into reserved ¼ cup wine mixture until cornstarch is dissolved. Add to **CROCK-POT**® slow cooker; stir until well blended. Cover; cook on HIGH 15 minutes or until thickened. Season with black pepper. Serve over mashed potatoes, if desired.

Makes 10 servings

Nutrition Information:
Serving Size about 1¼ cups, **Calories** 260, **Total Fat** 11g, **Saturated Fat** 3g, **Protein** 29g, **Carbohydrate** 10g, **Cholesterol** 65mg, **Dietary Fiber** 2g, **Sodium** 350mg

Horseradish Roast Beef and Potatoes

1   tablespoon freshly grated horseradish

1   tablespoon Dijon mustard

1   tablespoon minced fresh Italian parsley

1   teaspoon dried thyme, basil or oregano

3   pounds lean beef roast*

1   to 2 pounds Yukon Gold potatoes, peeled and quartered

1   pound mushrooms, chopped

2   cans (about 10 ounces *each*) fat-free reduced-sodium beef broth

2   large tomatoes, seeded and diced

1   large onion, sliced

1   green bell pepper, chopped

1   red bell pepper, chopped

1   cup dry red wine

3   cloves garlic, minced

1   whole bay leaf

*Unless you have a 5-, 6- or 7-quart **CROCK-POT®** slow cooker, cut any roast larger than 2½ pounds in half so it cooks completely.*

1. Combine horseradish, mustard, parsley and thyme in small bowl. Place roast in **CROCK-POT®** slow cooker and spread paste over roast.

2. Add potatoes, mushrooms, broth, tomatoes, onion, bell peppers, wine, garlic and bay leaf to **CROCK-POT®** slow cooker. Add enough water to cover roast and vegetables. Cover; cook on HIGH 2 hours. Turn **CROCK-POT®** slow cooker to LOW. Cover; cook on LOW 4 to 6 hours. Remove and discard bay leaf. Shred beef into 1-inch pieces before serving.

Makes 12 servings

Nutrition Information:
Serving Size ½ cup, **Calories** 220, **Total Fat** 5g, **Saturated Fat** 2g, **Protein** 28g, **Carbohydrate** 13g, **Cholesterol** 50mg, **Dietary Fiber** 2g, **Sodium** 210mg

Hearty Beef Short Ribs

1 large yellow onion, diced

⅓ cup canned crushed tomatoes

⅓ cup dry red wine

⅓ cup balsamic vinegar

2 carrots, diced

2 stalks celery, diced

3 cloves garlic, minced

3 whole bay leaves

1½ pounds beef flanken-style short ribs, bone-in

1 tablespoon black pepper

2¼ teaspoons coarse salt

1 tablespoon olive oil

TIP

For a change of pace from ordinary short rib recipes, ask your butcher for flanken-style beef short ribs. Flanken-style ribs are cut across the bones into wide, flat portions. They provide all the meaty flavor of the more common English-style short ribs with smaller, more manageable bones.

1. Combine onion, tomatoes, wine, vinegar, carrots, celery, garlic and bay leaves in **CROCK-POT®** slow cooker; stir to blend.

2. Season ribs with pepper and salt. Heat oil in large skillet over medium-high heat. Add ribs; cook 2 to 3 minutes on each side or just until browned. Remove to **CROCK-POT®** slow cooker.

3. Cover; cook on LOW 8 to 9 hours or on HIGH 5½ to 6 hours, turning once or twice, until meat is tender and falling off the bone. Remove ribs to large serving platter. Remove and discard bay leaves. Pour sauce into food processor or blender; process to desired consistency. Pour sauce evenly over ribs to serve.

Makes 8 servings

Nutrition Information:
Serving Size 3 ounces ribs with about ½ cup sauce, **Calories** 202, **Total Fat** 11g, **Saturated Fat** 4g, **Protein** 17g, **Carbohydrate** 7g, **Cholesterol** 50mg, **Dietary Fiber** 1g, **Sodium** 632mg

Slow Cooker Steak Fajitas

1   lean beef flank steak (about 1 pound)

1   medium onion, cut into strips

½   cup medium salsa, plus additional for garnish

2   tablespoons chopped fresh cilantro

2   tablespoons fresh lime juice

2   cloves garlic, minced

1   tablespoon chili powder

1   teaspoon ground cumin

½   teaspoon salt

1   small green bell pepper, cut into strips

1   small red bell pepper, cut into strips

8   (8-inch) flour tortillas, warmed

TIP

CROCK-POT® slow cooker recipes calling for raw meats should cook a minimum of 3 hours on LOW for food safety reasons. When in doubt, use an instant-read thermometer to ensure the meat has reached the recommended internal temperature for safe consumption.

1. Cut flank steak lengthwise in half, then crosswise into thin strips; place beef in **CROCK-POT®** slow cooker. Combine onion, ½ cup salsa, cilantro, lime juice, garlic, chili powder, cumin and salt in **CROCK-POT®** slow cooker. Cover; cook on LOW 5 to 6 hours.

2. Add bell peppers. Cover; cook on LOW 1 hour. Divide mixture evenly among tortillas. Serve with additional salsa, if desired.

Makes 4 servings

Nutrition Information:
Serving Size 2 fajitas
Calories 200
Total Fat 7g
Saturated Fat 3g
Protein 26g
Carbohydrate 9g
Cholesterol 35mg
Dietary Fiber 2g
Sodium 490mg

Meatballs and Spaghetti Sauce

- 2 pounds 95% lean ground beef
- 1 cup seasoned dry bread crumbs
- 1 medium yellow onion, chopped
- 2 eggs, beaten
- ¼ cup minced fresh Italian parsley
- 3 cloves garlic, minced and divided
- ½ teaspoon dry mustard
- ½ teaspoon black pepper
- 3 tablespoons olive oil, divided
- 1 can (about 28 ounces) whole tomatoes
- ½ cup chopped fresh basil, plus additional for garnish
- 1 teaspoon sugar

  Hot cooked spaghetti (optional)

1. Combine beef, bread crumbs, onion, eggs, parsley, 1 clove garlic, dry mustard and pepper in large bowl. Form into walnut-sized meatballs. Heat 1 tablespoon oil in large skillet over medium heat. Add meatballs; cook 6 to 8 minutes or until browned on all sides. Remove to **CROCK-POT**® slow cooker using slotted spoon.

2. Combine tomatoes, ½ cup basil, remaining 2 tablespoons oil, remaining 2 cloves garlic and sugar in medium bowl. Pour over meatballs, stirring to coat. Cover; cook on LOW 3 to 5 hours or on HIGH 2 to 4 hours. Serve over spaghetti, if desired. Garnish with additional basil.

Makes 8 servings

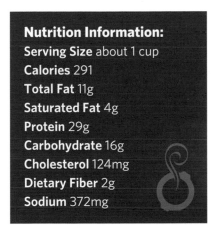

Nutrition Information:
Serving Size about 1 cup
Calories 291
Total Fat 11g
Saturated Fat 4g
Protein 29g
Carbohydrate 16g
Cholesterol 124mg
Dietary Fiber 2g
Sodium 372mg

Asian Beef with Mandarin Oranges

2 tablespoons vegetable oil

2 pounds lean boneless beef chuck roast, cut into ½-inch strips

1 small yellow onion, thinly sliced

1 head (about 5 ounces) bok choy, cleaned and chopped

1 can (5 ounces) sliced water chestnuts, drained

⅓ cup reduced-sodium soy sauce

1 package (about 3 ounces) shiitake mushrooms, sliced

1 small green bell pepper, sliced

2 teaspoons minced fresh ginger

¼ teaspoon salt

1 can (11 ounces) mandarin oranges in light syrup, drained and syrup reserved

2 tablespoons cornstarch

2 cups fat-free beef broth

6 cups hot cooked rice

1. Heat oil in large skillet over medium-high heat. Add beef in batches; cook and stir 6 to 8 minutes or until browned all sides. Remove to **CROCK-POT**® slow cooker using slotted spoon.

2. Add onion to same skillet; cook and stir over medium heat 3 to 5 minutes or until softened. Add bok choy, water chestnuts, soy sauce, mushrooms, bell pepper, ginger and salt; cook and stir 5 minutes or until bok choy is wilted. Spoon mixture over beef.

3. Stir reserved mandarin orange syrup into cornstarch in medium bowl until smooth. Whisk in broth; pour into **CROCK-POT**® slow cooker. Cover; cook on LOW 10 hours or on HIGH 5 to 6 hours.

4. Stir in mandarin oranges. Spoon 1 cup rice into each serving bowl; spoon ½ cup beef mixture over rice.

Makes 6 servings

Nutrition Information:
Serving Size about ½ cup beef mixture over 1 cup rice, **Calories** 409, **Total Fat** 12g, **Saturated Fat** 3g, **Protein** 29g, **Carbohydrate** 47g, **Cholesterol** 65mg, **Dietary Fiber** 2g, **Sodium** 717mg

Sauvignon Blanc Beef with Beets and Thyme

1 **pound red or yellow beets, quartered**

1 **tablespoon extra virgin olive oil**

3 **pounds lean boneless beef chuck roast***

1 **medium yellow onion, quartered**

2 **cloves garlic, minced**

5 **sprigs fresh thyme**

1 **whole bay leaf**

2 **whole cloves**

1 **cup fat-free chicken broth**

1 **cup Sauvignon Blanc or other dry white wine**

2 **tablespoons tomato paste**

  Salt and black pepper (optional)

Unless you have a 5-, 6- or 7-quart **CROCK-POT® slow cooker, cut any roast larger than 2½ pounds in half so it cooks completely.*

1. Layer beets evenly in **CROCK-POT**® slow cooker.

2. Heat oil in large skillet over medium heat. Add roast; cook 4 to 5 minutes or until browned on all sides. Add onion and garlic during last few minutes of browning. Remove to **CROCK-POT**® slow cooker. Add thyme, bay leaf and cloves.

3. Combine broth, wine and tomato paste in medium bowl; stir until blended. Season with salt and pepper, if desired. Pour over roast and beets. Cover; cook on LOW 8 to 10 hours. Remove and discard bay leaf.

Makes 6 servings

Nutrition Information:
Serving Size about 1¼ cups, **Calories** 400, **Total Fat** 12g, **Saturated Fat** 4g, **Protein** 52g, **Carbohydrate** 11g, **Cholesterol** 100mg, **Dietary Fiber** 3g, **Sodium** 386mg

Braised Chipotle Beef

- 2 tablespoons vegetable oil, divided
- 3 pounds lean boneless beef chuck roast, cut into 2-inch pieces
- 1 large yellow onion, cut into 1-inch pieces
- 2 red bell peppers, cut into 1-inch pieces
- 3 tablespoons tomato paste
- 1 tablespoon chipotle chili powder*
- 1 tablespoon paprika
- 1 tablespoon ground cumin
- 1 tablespoon minced garlic
- 1½ teaspoons salt
- 1 teaspoon dried oregano
- ½ teaspoon black pepper
- 1 cup fat-free beef broth
- 1 can (about 14 ounces) diced tomatoes, drained
- Hot cooked rice (optional)

*You may substitute conventional chili powder.

1. Heat 1 tablespoon oil in large skillet over medium-high heat. Add beef in batches; cook and stir 6 to 8 minutes or until browned on all sides. Remove to **CROCK-POT**® slow cooker.

2. Return skillet to medium heat. Add remaining 1 tablespoon oil and onion; cook and stir 3 to 5 minutes or until onion is softened. Add bell peppers; cook 2 minutes. Stir in tomato paste, chili powder, paprika, cumin, garlic, salt, oregano and black pepper; cook and stir 1 minute. Remove to **CROCK-POT**® slow cooker.

3. Return skillet to heat. Add broth, scraping up any browned bits from skillet. Pour over beef in **CROCK-POT**® slow cooker. Stir in tomatoes. Cover; cook on LOW 7 hours. Turn off heat. Let stand 5 minutes; skim fat from sauce. Serve over rice, if desired.

Makes 8 servings

Nutrition Information:
Serving Size about 1 cup, **Calories** 306, **Total Fat** 11g, **Saturated Fat** 3g, **Protein** 40g, **Carbohydrate** 9g, **Cholesterol** 75mg, **Dietary Fiber** 2g, **Sodium** 789mg

Corned Beef and Cabbage HF GF

12 small new potatoes, quartered

 4 carrots, sliced

 1 beef brisket (about 2 pounds)

 1 head cabbage, cut into wedges

 2 medium yellow onions, sliced

 3 whole bay leaves

 8 whole black peppercorns

 ½ teaspoon pickling spice

1. Place potatoes and carrots in bottom of **CROCK-POT®** slow cooker. Add beef, cabbage, onions, bay leaves, peppercorns, pickling spice and enough water to cover brisket. Cover; cook on LOW 4 to 5 hours or on HIGH 2 to 2½ hours.

2. Remove brisket to cutting board. Cover loosely with foil; let stand 10 to 15 minutes before slicing. Remove and discard bay leaves. Serve with vegetables.

Makes 10 servings

Nutrition Information:

Serving Size 3 ounces beef brisket with ½ cup vegetables
Calories 329
Total Fat 7g
Saturated Fat 2g
Protein 24g
Carbohydrate 42g
Cholesterol 56mg
Dietary Fiber 7g
Sodium 352mg

Beef with Green Chiles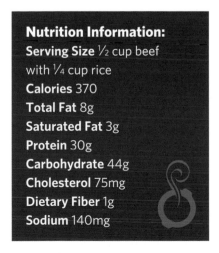

¼ **cup plus 1 tablespoon all-purpose flour, divided**

¼ **teaspoon black pepper**

1 **pound cubed beef stew meat**

1 **tablespoon vegetable oil**

2 **cloves garlic, minced**

1 **cup fat-free reduced-sodium beef broth**

1 **can (7 ounces) diced mild green chiles, drained**

½ **teaspoon dried oregano**

2 **tablespoons water**

1½ **cups hot cooked rice**

½ **cup diced tomato**

Use 2 cans of chiles for a slightly hotter flavor.

1. Combine ¼ cup flour and pepper in large bowl; stir to blend. Add beef; toss to coat. Heat oil in large skillet over medium-high heat. Add beef and garlic; cook and stir 6 to 8 minutes or until beef is browned on all sides. Remove beef mixture to **CROCK-POT®** slow cooker using slotted spoon. Add broth to skillet, stirring to scrape up any browned bits. Pour broth mixture into **CROCK-POT®** slow cooker. Add green chiles and oregano.

2. Cover; cook on LOW 7 to 8 hours. Turn **CROCK-POT®** slow cooker to HIGH. Stir water into remaining 1 tablespoon flour in small bowl until smooth. Whisk into **CROCK-POT®** slow cooker. Cover; cook on HIGH 15 minutes or until thickened. Serve over rice and top with tomato.

Makes 6 servings

Nutrition Information:
Serving Size ½ cup beef with ¼ cup rice
Calories 370
Total Fat 8g
Saturated Fat 3g
Protein 30g
Carbohydrate 44g
Cholesterol 75mg
Dietary Fiber 1g
Sodium 140mg

PERFECT POULTRY PLATES

Provençal Lemon and Olive Chicken

- 2 cups chopped onion
- 6 skinless chicken thighs (about 2 pounds)
- 1 medium lemon, thinly sliced and seeds removed
- ½ cup pitted green olives
- 1 tablespoon white vinegar or olive brine from jar
- 2 teaspoons herbes de Provence
- 1 whole bay leaf
- ⅛ teaspoon black pepper
- 1 cup fat-free reduced-sodium chicken broth
- ½ cup minced fresh Italian parsley

1. Place onion in **CROCK-POT**® slow cooker. Arrange chicken thighs over onion. Place lemon slice on each thigh. Add olives, vinegar, herbes de Provence, bay leaf and pepper; slowly pour in broth.

2. Cover; cook on LOW 5 to 6 hours or on HIGH 3 to 3½ hours. Remove and discard bay leaf. Stir in parsley.

Makes 6 servings

Nutrition Information:
Serving Size 1 chicken thigh with about ¾ cup olive mixture, **Calories** 140, **Total Fat** 6g, **Saturated Fat** 1g, **Protein** 14g, **Carbohydrate** 7g, **Cholesterol** 65mg, **Dietary Fiber** 2g, **Sodium** 430mg

Indian-Style Apricot Chicken

6 **skinless chicken thighs, rinsed and patted dry (about 2 pounds)**

¼ **teaspoon salt**

¼ **teaspoon black pepper**

1 **tablespoon vegetable oil**

1 **large onion, chopped**

2 **cloves garlic, minced**

2 **tablespoons grated fresh ginger**

½ **teaspoon ground cinnamon**

⅛ **teaspoon ground allspice**

1 **can (about 14 ounces) diced tomatoes**

1 **cup fat-free reduced-sodium chicken broth**

½ **(8-ounce) package dried apricots**

1 **pinch saffron threads (optional)**

Hot cooked rice (optional)

2 **tablespoons chopped fresh Italian parsley (optional)**

To skin chicken easily, grasp skin with paper towel and pull away. Repeat with fresh paper towel for each piece of chicken, discarding skins and towels.

1. Coat inside of **CROCK-POT®** slow cooker with nonstick cooking spray. Season chicken with salt and pepper. Heat oil in large skillet over medium-high heat. Add chicken; cook 6 to 8 minutes or until browned on all sides. Remove to **CROCK-POT®** slow cooker using slotted spoon.

2. Add onion to skillet; cook and stir 3 to 5 minutes or until translucent. Stir in garlic, ginger, cinnamon and allspice; cook and stir 15 to 30 seconds or until mixture is fragrant. Add tomatoes and broth; cook 2 to 3 minutes or until mixture is heated through. Pour into **CROCK-POT®** slow cooker.

3. Add apricots and saffron, if desired. Cover; cook on LOW 5 to 6 hours or on HIGH 3 to 4 hours. Serve with rice, if desired. Garnish with parsley.

Makes 6 servings

Nutrition Information:
Serving Size 1 chicken thigh with about ½ cup sauce, **Calories** 210, **Total Fat** 5g, **Saturated Fat** 1g, **Protein** 15g, **Carbohydrate** 26g, **Cholesterol** 65mg, **Dietary Fiber** 4g, **Sodium** 400mg

Lemon and Herb Turkey Breast ⓛⒻ ⒼⒻ

1 split turkey breast (about 3 pounds)

½ cup lemon juice

½ cup dry white wine

6 cloves garlic, minced

¼ teaspoon salt

¼ teaspoon dried parsley flakes

¼ teaspoon dried tarragon

¼ teaspoon dried rosemary

¼ teaspoon dried sage

¼ teaspoon black pepper

Sprigs fresh sage and rosemary (optional)

Lemon slices (optional)

Place turkey in **CROCK-POT®** slow cooker. Combine lemon juice, wine, garlic, salt, parsley flakes, tarragon, rosemary, sage and pepper in medium bowl; stir to blend. Pour lemon juice mixture over turkey in **CROCK-POT®** slow cooker. Cover; cook on LOW 8 to 10 hours or on HIGH 4 to 5 hours. Garnish with fresh sage, fresh rosemary and lemon slices.

Makes 4 servings

Nutrition Information:
Serving Size 3 ounces turkey
Calories 320
Total Fat 2g
Saturated Fat 1g
Protein 64g
Carbohydrate 4g
Cholesterol 175mg
Dietary Fiber 0g
Sodium 260mg

Chicken Scaloppine in Alfredo Sauce

- **2** tablespoons all-purpose flour
- **¼** teaspoon salt
- **¼** teaspoon black pepper
- **6** boneless, skinless chicken tenderloins (about 1 pound), cut lengthwise in half
- **1** tablespoon butter
- **1** tablespoon olive oil
- **1** cup Alfredo pasta sauce
- **1** package (12 ounces) uncooked spinach noodles

1. Place flour, salt and pepper in large bowl; stir to combine. Add chicken; toss to coat. Heat butter and oil in large skillet over medium-high heat. Add chicken; cook 3 minutes per side or until browned. Remove chicken in single layer to **CROCK-POT**® slow cooker.

2. Add Alfredo pasta sauce to **CROCK-POT**® slow cooker. Cover; cook on LOW 1 to 1½ hours.

3. Meanwhile, cook noodles according to package directions. Drain; place in large shallow bowl. Spoon chicken and sauce over noodles.

Makes 6 servings

Nutrition Information:
Serving Size 1 chicken tenderloin with ¼ cup sauce and ¼ cup noodles
Calories 380
Total Fat 11g
Saturated Fat 5g
Protein 27g
Carbohydrate 45g
Cholesterol 65mg
Dietary Fiber 2g
Sodium 500mg

Greek Chicken Pitas with Creamy Mustard Sauce

Filling

1 medium green bell pepper, sliced into ½-inch strips

1 medium onion, cut into 8 wedges

2 pounds boneless, skinless chicken breasts, rinsed and patted dry (about ½ pound)

1 tablespoon extra virgin olive oil

2 teaspoons Greek seasoning

Sauce

¼ cup nonfat plain yogurt

¼ cup fat-free mayonnaise

1 tablespoon prepared mustard

4 (6½-inch) whole pita bread rounds, cut in half

½ cup reduced-fat crumbled feta cheese

Optional toppings: sliced cucumbers, sliced tomatoes and/or kalamata olives

1. Coat inside of **CROCK-POT®** slow cooker with nonstick cooking spray. Place bell pepper and onion in bottom. Add chicken; drizzle with oil. Sprinkle evenly with Greek seasoning. Cover; cook on HIGH 1¾ hours or until chicken is no longer pink in center and vegetables are crisp-tender.

2. Whisk yogurt, mayonnaise and mustard in small bowl until smooth. Remove chicken to cutting board and slice. Remove vegetables using slotted spoon. Fill pita halves evenly with chicken, yogurt sauce, vegetables and feta cheese. Top as desired.

Makes 8 servings

Nutrition Information:
Serving Size 1 pita half, **Calories** 170, **Total Fat** 8g, **Saturated Fat** 5g, **Protein** 11g, **Carbohydrate** 21g, **Cholesterol** 20mg, **Dietary Fiber** 2g, **Sodium** 400mg

Japanese-Style Simmered Chicken Thighs and Vegetables

3 medium carrots, cut into 2-inch pieces

½ pound shiitake mushrooms, stemmed and quartered

1 medium onion, cut into 1-inch pieces

1 medium Japanese eggplant, halved lengthwise and cut into ½-inch-thick slices

8 boneless, skinless chicken thighs (about 2½ pounds)

½ cup reduced-sodium soy sauce

½ cup sugar

⅓ cup chicken broth

¼ cup mirin

1 tablespoon cornstarch

1 teaspoon grated fresh ginger

1 teaspoon minced garlic

¼ teaspoon Chinese five-spice powder

Hot cooked rice (optional)

1. Place carrots, mushrooms, onion and eggplant in **CROCK-POT**® slow cooker. Top with chicken thighs; set aside.

2. Combine soy sauce, sugar, broth, mirin, cornstarch, ginger, garlic and five-spice powder in small saucepan; cook and stir over medium heat until sugar dissolves and mixture thickens slightly. Pour over chicken and vegetables. Cover; cook on LOW 7 hours. Serve chicken thighs, vegetables and sauce over rice, if desired.

Makes 8 servings

Nutrition Information:
Serving Size 1 chicken thigh with ¾ cup sauce and vegetables, **Calories** 230, **Total Fat** 8g, **Saturated Fat** 3g, **Protein** 24g, **Carbohydrate** 23g, **Cholesterol** 90mg, **Dietary Fiber** 4g, **Sodium** 660mg

Chipotle Turkey Sloppy Joe Sliders

1 **pound turkey Italian sausage, casings removed**

1 **package (14 ounces) frozen green and red bell pepper strips with onions**

1 **can (6 ounces) tomato paste**

1 **tablespoon quick-cooking tapioca**

1 **tablespoon minced canned chipotle pepper in adobo sauce, plus 1 tablespoon sauce**

2 **teaspoons ground cumin**

½ **teaspoon dried thyme**

12 **corn muffins, split**

1. Brown sausage in large skillet over medium-high heat 6 to 8 minutes, stirring to break up meat. Drain fat. Remove to **CROCK-POT®** slow cooker.

2. Stir in pepper strips with onions, tomato paste, tapioca, chipotle pepper and sauce, cumin and thyme. Cover; cook on LOW 8 to 10 hours. Spoon sausage mixture evenly into corn muffins.

Makes 6 servings

Nutrition Information:
Serving Size 2 sliders
Calories 180
Total Fat 6g
Saturated Fat 2g
Protein 16g
Carbohydrate 10g
Cholesterol 60mg
Dietary Fiber 2g
Sodium 500mg

Slow Cooker Turkey Breast ⓛⒻ Ⓛⓢ ⒼⒻ

1 turkey breast (3 pounds)*

Garlic powder

Paprika

Dried parsley flakes

Unless you have a 5-, 6- or 7-quart **CROCK-POT® slow cooker, cut any meat larger than 2½ pounds in half so it cooks completely.*

1. Season turkey with garlic powder, paprika and parsley flakes. Place in **CROCK-POT**® slow cooker. Cover; cook on LOW 6 to 8 hours.

2. Remove turkey to cutting board. Cover loosely with foil; let stand 10 to 15 minutes before slicing into six pieces.

Makes 6 servings

Nutrition Information:
Serving Size 1 piece turkey
Calories 240
Total Fat 3g
Saturated Fat 1g
Protein 53g
Carbohydrate 0g
Cholesterol 111mg
Dietary Fiber 0g
Sodium 122mg

Cuban-Style Curried Turkey ⊞

2 tablespoons all-purpose flour

½ teaspoon salt

¼ teaspoon black pepper

1 pound boneless turkey breast or turkey tenderloins, cut into 1-inch cubes

2 tablespoons vegetable oil, divided

1 small yellow onion, chopped

1 clove garlic, minced

1 can (about 15 ounces) reduced-sodium black beans, rinsed and drained

1 can (about 14 ounces) no-salt-added diced tomatoes

½ cup fat-free reduced-sodium chicken broth

⅓ cup raisins

¼ teaspoon curry powder

⅛ teaspoon red pepper flakes

1 tablespoon lime juice

2 cups hot cooked rice (optional)

1 tablespoon minced fresh cilantro (optional)

1 tablespoon minced green onion (optional)

1. Combine flour, salt and black pepper in large resealable food storage bag. Add turkey; shake to coat. Heat 1 tablespoon oil in large skillet over medium heat. Add turkey; cook 6 to 8 minutes or until browned on both sides. Remove to **CROCK-POT®** slow cooker.

2. Heat remaining 1 tablespoon oil in same skillet over medium heat. Add onion; cook and stir 3 minutes or until tender. Stir in garlic; cook 30 seconds. Remove to **CROCK-POT®** slow cooker.

3. Stir in beans, tomatoes, broth, raisins, curry powder and red pepper flakes. Cover; cook on LOW 4 to 6 hours. Stir in lime juice. Serve over rice, if desired. Garnish with cilantro and green onion.

Makes 4 servings

Nutrition Information:
Serving Size about 1¾ cups, **Calories** 328, **Total Fat** 8g, **Saturated Fat** 1g, **Protein** 32g, **Carbohydrate** 34g, **Cholesterol** 56mg, **Dietary Fiber** 6g, **Sodium** 690mg

Curry Chicken with Mango and Red Pepper

6 boneless, skinless chicken breasts (about 2 pounds)

Salt and black pepper (optional)

Nonstick cooking spray

1 bag (8 ounces) frozen mango pieces, thawed and drained

2 red bell peppers, diced

⅓ cup raisins

1 shallot, thinly sliced

¾ cup fat-free reduced-sodium chicken broth

1 tablespoon cider vinegar

2 cloves garlic, crushed

4 thin slices fresh ginger

1 teaspoon ground cumin

½ teaspoon curry powder

½ teaspoon whole cloves

¼ teaspoon ground red pepper (optional)

3 cups hot cooked rice

Fresh cilantro (optional)

1. Season chicken with salt and black pepper, if desired. Spray large skillet with cooking spray; heat over medium heat. Add chicken; cook 3 minutes per side or until lightly browned. Remove to **CROCK-POT**® slow cooker.

2. Add mango, bell peppers, raisins and shallot to **CROCK-POT**® slow cooker. Combine broth, vinegar, garlic, ginger, cumin, curry powder, cloves and ground red pepper, if desired, in small bowl; pour over chicken. Cover; cook on LOW 6 to 8 hours or on HIGH 3 to 4 hours. Serve chicken over rice topped with mangos, raisins and cooking liquid. Garnish with cilantro.

Makes 6 servings

Nutrition Information:
Serving Size 1 chicken breast with ½ cup mango mixture and sauce and ½ cup rice, **Calories** 320, **Total Fat** 4g, **Saturated Fat** 1g, **Protein** 29g, **Carbohydrate** 41g, **Cholesterol** 75mg, **Dietary Fiber** 3g, **Sodium** 210mg

Braised Italian Chicken with Tomatoes and Olives

4 boneless, skinless chicken breasts (1½ pounds)

¼ teaspoon kosher salt

½ teaspoon black pepper

½ cup all-purpose flour

Nonstick cooking spray

1 can (about 14 ounces) no-salt-added diced tomatoes, drained

⅓ cup dry red wine

⅓ cup quartered pitted kalamata olives

1 clove garlic, minced

1 teaspoon chopped fresh rosemary

½ teaspoon red pepper flakes

Hot cooked linguini or spaghetti (optional)

Grated Parmesan cheese (optional)

Sprigs fresh rosemary (optional)

1. Season chicken with salt and black pepper. Place flour on shallow plate. Add chicken; turn to coat.

2. Heat cooking spray in large skillet over medium heat. Add chicken in batches; cook 6 to 8 minutes or until browned on both sides. Remove to **CROCK-POT**® slow cooker using slotted spoon. Add tomatoes, wine, olives and garlic. Cover; cook on LOW 4 to 5 hours.

3. Stir in chopped rosemary and red pepper flakes. Cover; cook on LOW 1 hour. Serve over linguini, if desired. Garnish with cheese and rosemary sprigs.

Makes 4 servings

Nutrition Information:
Serving Size 1 chicken breast with ½ cup sauce, **Calories** 374, **Total Fat** 7g, **Saturated Fat** 1g, **Protein** 51g, **Carbohydrate** 18g, **Cholesterol** 145mg, **Dietary Fiber** 1g, **Sodium** 808mg

Turkey Piccata

2½ tablespoons all-purpose flour

¼ teaspoon salt

¼ teaspoon black pepper

1 pound turkey breast, cut into strips

1 tablespoon unsalted butter

1 tablespoon olive oil

½ cup fat-free reduced-sodium chicken broth

   Grated peel of 1 lemon

2 teaspoons lemon juice

2 cups hot cooked rice

2 tablespoons finely chopped fresh Italian parsley

1. Combine flour, salt and pepper in large resealable food storage bag. Add turkey; shake to coat. Heat butter and oil in large skillet over medium-high heat. Add turkey; cook and stir 3 to 5 minutes or until browned on all sides. Arrange in single layer in **CROCK-POT®** slow cooker.

2. Pour broth into skillet, scraping up any browned bits from skillet. Pour into **CROCK-POT®** slow cooker. Add lemon peel and juice. Cover; cook on LOW 2 hours. Serve over rice. Sprinkle with parsley.

Makes 4 servings

Nutrition Information:
Serving Size about 4 ounces turkey breast with ¼ cup sauce and ½ cup rice
Calories 350
Total Fat 7g
Saturated Fat 3g
Protein 37g
Carbohydrate 31g
Cholesterol 100mg
Dietary Fiber 1g
Sodium 260mg

Sauced Little Smokies

- **1 bottle (14 ounces) barbecue sauce**
- **¾ cup grape jelly**
- **½ cup packed brown sugar**
- **½ cup reduced-sodium ketchup**
- **1 tablespoon prepared mustard**
- **1 teaspoon Worcestershire sauce**
- **3 packages (14 to 16 ounces *each*) miniature turkey hot dogs**

Stir barbecue sauce, jelly, brown sugar, ketchup, mustard and Worcestershire sauce into **CROCK-POT®** slow cooker until combined. Add hot dogs; stir to coat. Cover; cook on LOW 3 to 4 hours or on HIGH 1 to 2 hours.

Makes 24 servings

Nutrition Information:
Serving Size 2 smokies
Calories 160
Total Fat 4g
Saturated Fat 2g
Protein 8g
Carbohydrate 23g
Cholesterol 25mg
Dietary Fiber 0g
Sodium 660mg

Autumn Herbed Chicken with Fennel and Squash

  6 **chicken thighs (about 3 pounds)**

  ½ **teaspoon salt**

  ½ **teaspoon black pepper**

  ½ **cup all-purpose flour**

  1 **tablespoon olive oil**

  1 **fennel bulb, thinly sliced**

  ½ **butternut squash, seeded and cut into ¾-inch cubes**

  1 **teaspoon dried thyme**

  ¾ **cup walnuts**

  ¾ **cup fat-free reduced-sodium chicken broth**

  ½ **cup unsweetened apple juice**

  3 **cups hot cooked wild rice**

  ¼ **cup fresh basil, sliced into ribbons (optional)**

  2 **teaspoons fresh rosemary, finely minced (optional)**

To reduce calories and fat even further, remove the skin of the chicken before eating.

1. Season chicken on all sides with salt and pepper, then lightly coat with flour. Heat oil in large skillet over medium heat. Working in batches, brown chicken 3 to 5 minutes on each side. Remove to **CROCK-POT**® slow cooker using slotted spoon.

2. Add fennel, squash and thyme. Stir well to combine. Add walnuts, if desired, broth and juice. Cover; cook on LOW 5 to 7 hours or on HIGH 2½ to 4½ hours.

3. Serve over rice, if desired. Garnish with basil and rosemary.

Makes 6 servings

Nutrition Information:
Serving Size 1 chicken breast with 1 cup vegetable mixture and ½ cup rice, **Calories** 340, **Total Fat** 14g, **Saturated Fat** 2g, **Protein** 20g, **Carbohydrate** 36g, **Cholesterol** 65mg, **Dietary Fiber** 4g, **Sodium** 330mg

Fusilli Pizzaiola with Turkey Meatballs ⓗⒻ

- **2** cans (about 14 ounces *each*) no-salt-added whole tomatoes
- **1** can (8 ounces) no-salt-added tomato sauce
- **¼** cup chopped yellow onion
- **¼** cup shredded carrot
- **2** tablespoons no-salt-added tomato paste
- **2** tablespoons chopped fresh basil
- **1** clove garlic, minced
- **½** teaspoon dried thyme
- **¼** teaspoon sugar
- **¼** teaspoon black pepper, divided
- **1** whole bay leaf
- **1** pound lean ground turkey
- **¼** cup Italian-seasoned dry bread crumbs
- **1** egg, lightly beaten
- **1** tablespoon fat-free (skim) milk
- **2** tablespoons chopped fresh Italian parsley
- **8** ounces fusilli or other spiral-shaped pasta, cooked and drained

1. Combine tomatoes, tomato sauce, onion, carrot, tomato paste, basil, garlic, thyme, sugar, ⅛ teaspoon pepper and bay leaf in **CROCK-POT®** slow cooker. Cover; cook on LOW 4½ to 5 hours.

2. Prepare meatballs 45 minutes before end of cooking. Preheat oven to 350°F. Spray large baking sheet with nonstick cooking spray. Combine turkey, bread crumbs, egg, milk, parsley and remaining ⅛ teaspoon pepper in large bowl; stir to blend. Shape mixture evenly into balls; arrange on prepared baking sheet. Bake 25 minutes or until no longer pink in center.

3. Turn **CROCK-POT®** slow cooker to HIGH. Add meatballs to **CROCK-POT®** slow cooker. Cover; cook on HIGH 45 minutes to 1 hour or until meatballs are heated through. Remove and discard bay leaf. Place pasta in large serving bowl; top with meatballs and sauce.

Makes 4 servings

Nutrition Information:
Serving Size about 1 cup sauce and 4 meatballs on ½ cup pasta, **Calories** 479, **Total Fat** 10g, **Saturated Fat** 3g, **Protein** 35g, **Carbohydrate** 65g, **Cholesterol** 119mg, **Dietary Fiber** 6g, **Sodium** 273mg

Slow-Cooked Chicken Fajitas

- **2** tablespoons olive oil
- **6** boneless, skinless chicken breasts (about 2 pounds), cut into thin strips
- **½** teaspoon salt
- **¼** teaspoon black pepper
- **½** medium red bell pepper, sliced
- **½** medium green bell pepper, sliced
- **½** medium yellow bell pepper, sliced
- **1** medium onion, sliced
- **¾** cup fat-free reduced-sodium chicken broth
- **1** tablespoon Worcestershire sauce
- **2** tablespoons all-purpose flour
- **2** teaspoons garlic powder
- **1** teaspoon ground cumin
- **1** teaspoon dried oregano
- **1** teaspoon paprika
- **⅛** teaspoon ground red pepper
- **14** grape tomatoes
- **2** tablespoons chopped fresh cilantro
- **1** tablespoon lime juice
- **12** (6-inch) corn tortillas, warmed

    Optional toppings: guacamole, sour cream and/or salsa

1. Heat 1 tablespoon oil in large skillet over medium-high heat. Sprinkle chicken with salt and pepper. Add half of chicken to skillet; cook 4 to 6 minutes or until browned, turning occasionally. Remove to large paper towel-lined plate. Repeat with remaining 1 tablespoon oil and chicken.

2. Add bell peppers and onion to **CROCK-POT®** slow cooker; top with chicken. Combine broth, Worcestershire sauce, flour, garlic powder, cumin, oregano, paprika and ground red pepper in medium bowl; stir to blend. Add broth mixture to **CROCK-POT®** slow cooker.

3. Cover; cook on LOW 8 to 9 hours or on HIGH 4 to 4½ hours. Stir in tomatoes 30 minutes before end of cooking. Turn off heat. Stir in cilantro and lime juice. Serve in tortillas. Top as desired.

Makes 6 servings

Nutrition Information:

Serving Size 2 fajitas with ½ cup filling, **Calories** 350, **Total Fat** 10g, **Saturated Fat** 2g, **Protein** 35g, **Carbohydrate** 29g, **Cholesterol** 95mg, **Dietary Fiber** 4g, **Sodium** 470mg

Spicy Turkey with Citrus au Jus LS GF

1 turkey breast (about 4 pounds)*

¼ cup (½ stick) unsalted butter, softened

Grated peel of 1 lemon

1 teaspoon chili powder

¼ to ½ teaspoon black pepper

⅛ to ¼ teaspoon red pepper flakes

1 tablespoon lemon juice

*Unless you have a 5-, 6- or 7-quart **CROCK-POT**® slow cooker, cut any meat larger than 2½ pounds in half so it cooks completely.

1. Coat inside of **CROCK-POT**® slow cooker with nonstick cooking spray. Add turkey breast.

2. Combine butter, lemon peel, chili powder, black pepper and red pepper flakes in small bowl; stir until well blended. Spread mixture over top and sides of turkey. Cover; cook on LOW 4 to 5 hours or on HIGH 2½ to 3 hours.

3. Remove turkey to cutting board. Cover loosely with foil; let stand 10 to 15 minutes before slicing. Turn off heat. Let cooking liquid stand 15 minutes. Strain liquid; discard solids. Stir lemon juice into cooking liquid. Serve sauce with turkey.

Makes 8 servings

Nutrition Information:

Serving Size 8 ounces turkey breast with 2 tablespoons sauce
Calories 304
Total Fat 7g
Saturated Fat 4g
Protein 56g
Carbohydrate 0g
Cholesterol 156mg
Dietary Fiber 0g
Sodium 115mg

Chicken Tangier

- **2 tablespoons dried oregano**
- **2 teaspoons seasoned salt**
- **2 teaspoons puréed garlic**
- **¼ teaspoon black pepper**
- **6 boneless, skinless chicken breasts (2 pounds)**
- **1 lemon, thinly sliced**
- **½ cup dry white wine**
- **2 tablespoons olive oil**
- **1 cup pitted prunes**
- **½ cup pitted green olives**
- **¼ cup raisins**
- **2 tablespoons capers**
- **Hot cooked couscous or rice (optional)**
- **Chopped fresh Italian parsley or cilantro (optional)**

It may seem like a lot, but this recipe really does call for 2 tablespoons dried oregano in order to more accurately represent the powerfully seasoned flavors of Morocco.

1. Stir oregano, salt, garlic and pepper in small bowl. Rub evenly onto chicken.

2. Coat inside of **CROCK-POT®** slow cooker with nonstick cooking spray. Arrange chicken with lemon slices between pieces. Pour wine over chicken; sprinkle with oil. Add prunes, olives, raisins and capers. Cover; cook on LOW 7 to 8 hours or on HIGH 4 to 5 hours. Serve over couscous, if desired. Garnish with parsley.

Makes 6 servings

Nutrition Information:
Serving Size 1 chicken breast with about ½ cup prune mixture
Calories 320
Total Fat 11g
Saturated Fat 2g
Protein 26g
Carbohydrate 26g
Cholesterol 75mg
Dietary Fiber 2g
Sodium 570mg

Mediterranean Chicken

- **1 tablespoon olive oil**
- **6 boneless, skinless chicken breasts (about 2 pounds)**
- **1 can (28 ounces) diced tomatoes**
- **2 medium yellow onions, chopped**
- **½ cup dry sherry**
- **Juice of 2 lemons**
- **2 tablespoons minced garlic**
- **2 cinnamon sticks**
- **1 whole bay leaf**
- **½ teaspoon black pepper**
- **1 pound cooked egg noodles**
- **½ cup feta cheese**

1. Heat oil in large skillet over medium-high heat. Add chicken; cook and stir 5 to 7 minutes or until browned on both sides.

2. Combine tomatoes, onions, sherry, lemon juice, garlic, cinnamon sticks, bay leaf and pepper in **CROCK-POT®** slow cooker. Add chicken. Cover; cook on LOW 8 to 10 hours or on HIGH 4 to 5 hours.

3. Remove and discard cinnamon sticks and bay leaf. Serve chicken and sauce over cooked noodles. Sprinkle each serving evenly with cheese.

Makes 8 servings

Nutrition Information:
Serving Size 1 cup chicken mixture on ½ cup pasta, **Calories** 432, **Total Fat** 8g, **Saturated Fat** 3g, **Protein** 34g, **Carbohydrate** 51g, **Cholesterol** 81mg, **Dietary Fiber** 3g, **Sodium** 440mg

Chicken Cacciatore

- **4** teaspoons olive oil
- **6** boneless, skinless chicken breasts (about 2 pounds)
- **½** teaspoon salt
- **¼** teaspoon black pepper
- **½** medium red bell pepper, sliced
- **½** medium green bell pepper, sliced
- **½** medium yellow bell pepper, sliced
- **1** cup onion, sliced
- **14** grape tomatoes
- **1½** cups water
- **¼** cup all-purpose flour
- **2** teaspoons garlic powder
- **1** teaspoon ground cumin
- **1** teaspoon dried oregano
- **1** teaspoon paprika
- **⅛** teaspoon ground red pepper
  Hot cooked noodles or rice (optional)

1. Heat 2 teaspoons oil in large skillet over medium-high heat. Sprinkle chicken with salt and black pepper. Add half of chicken to skillet; cook 4 minutes per side or until browned. Remove to large plate. Repeat with remaining 2 teaspoons oil and chicken.

2. Add bell peppers, onion and grape tomatoes to **CROCK-POT**® slow cooker. Combine water, flour, garlic powder, cumin, oregano, paprika and ground red pepper in medium bowl; mix well. Add to **CROCK-POT**® slow cooker. Top with chicken. Cover; cook on LOW 8 to 9 hours or on HIGH 4 to 4½ hours. Serve over noodles, if desired.

Makes 6 servings

Nutrition Information:
Serving Size 1 chicken breast with ½ cup sauce, **Calories** 330, **Total Fat** 9g, **Saturated Fat** 2g, **Protein** 50g, **Carbohydrate** 10g, **Cholesterol** 145mg, **Dietary Fiber** 2g, **Sodium** 460mg

Turkey Spinach Lasagna

Nonstick cooking spray

¾ cup chopped onion

2 medium cloves garlic, minced

1 pound lean ground turkey

1 teaspoon Italian seasoning

¼ teaspoon black pepper

1 container (15 ounces) fat-free ricotta cheese

1 cup (4 ounces) reduced-fat Italian shredded cheese blend, divided

12 ounces no-boil lasagna noodles

1 package (10 ounces) frozen chopped spinach, thawed and pressed dry

1 jar (24 ounces) chunky marinara sauce

½ cup water

1. Spray large skillet with cooking spray; heat over medium heat. Add onion and garlic; cook and stir 4 minutes. Add turkey; cook and stir until no longer pink, stirring to break up meat. Season with Italian seasoning and pepper; remove from heat. Set aside.

2. Combine ricotta cheese and ½ cup Italian cheese in small bowl; mix well.

3. Layer half of uncooked noodles, breaking in half to fit and overlap as necessary, in **CROCK-POT®** slow cooker. Spread half of meat mixture and half of spinach over noodles. Top with half of marinara sauce and ¼ cup water. Gently spread cheese mixture on top. Continue layering with remaining noodles, meat mixture, spinach, marinara sauce and ¼ cup water.

4. Cover; cook on LOW 4 hours. To serve, sprinkle top with remaining ½ cup Italian cheese. Cover; cook on LOW 10 to 15 minutes or until cheese is melted. Cut evenly into eight squares.

Makes 8 servings

Nutrition Information:
Serving Size 1 square, **Calories** 370, **Total Fat** 8g, **Saturated Fat** 3g, **Protein** 30g, **Carbohydrate** 43g, **Cholesterol** 85mg, **Dietary Fiber** 2g, **Sodium** 530mg

Sesame Chicken

- 1 cup rice flour
- 3 tablespoons sesame seeds
- 1 teaspoon black pepper
- 6 boneless, skinless chicken breasts (about 2 pounds)
- 2 tablespoons vegetable oil
- 1 cup fat-free reduced-sodium chicken broth
- ½ cup chopped celery
- ¼ cup chopped onion
- 1 teaspoon dried tarragon
- 2 tablespoons water
- 2 tablespoons cornstarch
  Hot cooked rice (optional)
  Squash ribbons (optional)

1. Combine rice flour, sesame seeds and pepper in large bowl; stir to blend. Add chicken; toss to coat.

2. Heat oil in large skillet over medium heat. Add chicken; cook 5 to 7 minutes or until browned on all sides. Remove to **CROCK-POT**® slow cooker using slotted spoon.

3. Add broth, celery, onion and tarragon to **CROCK-POT**® slow cooker. Cover; cook on LOW 7 to 8 hours or on HIGH 3 to 4 hours.

4. Stir water into cornstarch in small bowl until smooth. Whisk cornstarch mixture into **CROCK-POT**® slow cooker. Cover; cook on HIGH 15 to 20 minutes or until thickened. Serve with rice and squash ribbons, if desired.

Makes 6 servings

Nutrition Information:
Serving Size 1 chicken breast with ¼ cup sauce, **Calories** 310, **Total Fat** 10g, **Saturated Fat** 2g, **Protein** 28g, **Carbohydrate** 25g, **Cholesterol** 75mg, **Dietary Fiber** 1g, **Sodium** 230mg

Turkey with Chunky Cherry Relish ⒧Ⓕ Ⓖ Ⓕ

- 1 bag (16 ounces) frozen dark cherries, coarsely chopped
- 1 can (about 14 ounces) diced tomatoes with jalapeños
- 1 package (6 ounces) dried cherries or dried cherry-flavored cranberries, coarsely chopped
- 2 small onions, thinly sliced
- 1 small green bell pepper, chopped
- ½ cup packed brown sugar
- 2 tablespoons quick-cooking tapioca
- 2 teaspoons salt
- ½ teaspoon ground cinnamon
- ½ teaspoon black pepper
- 1 bone-in turkey breast (about 2 pounds)
- 2 tablespoons water
- 1 tablespoon cornstarch

1. Place frozen cherries, tomatoes, dried cherries, onions, bell pepper, brown sugar, tapioca, salt, cinnamon and black pepper in **CROCK-POT®** slow cooker; stir to blend.

2. Place turkey on top of mixture. Cover; cook on LOW 7 to 8 hours. Remove turkey from **CROCK-POT®** slow cooker; keep warm.

3. Turn **CROCK-POT®** slow cooker to HIGH. Stir water into cornstarch in small bowl until smooth. Whisk into cherry mixture. Cook, uncovered, on HIGH 15 minutes or until sauce is thickened. Slice turkey and top with relish.

Makes 8 servings

Nutrition Information:
Serving Size 4 ounces turkey with 1 cup relish, **Calories** 300, **Total Fat** 2g, **Saturated Fat** 1g, **Protein** 29g, **Carbohydrate** 44g, **Cholesterol** 55mg, **Dietary Fiber** 4g, **Sodium** 670mg

GREAT-TASTING SIDES

Braised Sweet and Sour Cabbage with Apples

- 2 tablespoons unsalted butter
- 6 cups coarsely shredded red cabbage
- 1 large sweet apple, peeled, cored and cut into 1-inch pieces
- 3 whole cloves
- ½ cup raisins
- ½ cup apple cider
- 3 tablespoons cider vinegar, divided
- 2 tablespoons packed dark brown sugar
- ½ teaspoon salt
- ¼ teaspoon black pepper

1. Melt butter in large skillet over medium heat. Add cabbage; cook and stir 3 minutes or until cabbage is glossy. Remove to **CROCK-POT®** slow cooker.

2. Add apple, cloves, raisins, apple cider, 2 tablespoons vinegar, brown sugar, salt and pepper. Cover; cook on LOW 2½ to 3 hours. Remove and discard cloves. Stir in remaining 1 tablespoon vinegar.

Makes 6 servings

Nutrition Information:
Serving Size about 1¼ cups, **Calories** 153, **Total Fat** 4g, **Saturated Fat** 2g, **Protein** 2g, **Carbohydrate** 29g, **Cholesterol** 10mg, **Dietary Fiber** 3g, **Sodium** 227mg

Slow-Roasted Potatoes   GF

16 small new potatoes

3 tablespoons unsalted butter, cut into small pieces

1 teaspoon paprika

½ teaspoon salt

½ teaspoon black pepper

¼ teaspoon garlic powder

1. Combine potatoes, butter, paprika, salt, pepper and garlic powder in **CROCK-POT®** slow cooker; stir to blend. Cover; cook on LOW 7 hours or on HIGH 4 hours.

2. Remove potatoes with slotted spoon to large serving dish; cover with foil to keep warm. Add 1 to 2 tablespoons water to cooking liquid and stir until well blended. Pour over potatoes.

Makes 8 servings

Nutrition Information:

Serving Size 2 potatoes

Calories 280

Total Fat 5g

Saturated Fat 3g

Protein 6g

Carbohydrate 54g

Cholesterol 10mg

Dietary Fiber 8g

Sodium 170mg

Creamy Curried Spinach

- **3 packages (10 ounces *each*) frozen spinach, thawed**
- **1 onion, chopped**
- **4 teaspoons minced garlic**
- **2 tablespoons curry powder**
- **1 tablespoon unsalted butter, melted**
- **¼ cup fat-free reduced-sodium chicken broth**
- **¼ cup light whipping cream**
- **1 teaspoon lemon juice**

Combine spinach, onion, garlic, curry powder, butter and broth in **CROCK-POT®** slow cooker. Cover; cook on LOW 3 to 4 hours or on HIGH 2 hours. Stir in cream and lemon juice 30 minutes before end of cooking time.

Makes 8 servings

Nutrition Information:
Serving Size about ¼ cup
Calories 80
Total Fat 5g
Saturated Fat 3g
Protein 4g
Carbohydrate 7g
Cholesterol 10mg
Dietary Fiber 4g
Sodium 110mg

Slow-Cooked Succotash LF V GF

2 teaspoons canola oil

1 cup chopped onion

1 cup chopped green bell pepper

1 cup chopped celery

1 teaspoon paprika

1½ cups frozen yellow or white corn

1½ cups frozen lima beans

1 cup canned reduced-sodium diced tomatoes

2 teaspoons dried parsley flakes *or* 1 tablespoon minced fresh Italian parsley

½ teaspoon salt

½ teaspoon black pepper

1. Heat oil in large skillet over medium heat. Add onion, bell pepper and celery; cook and stir 5 minutes or until vegetables are crisp-tender. Stir in paprika.

2. Combine onion mixture, corn, beans, tomatoes, parsley flakes, salt and black pepper in **CROCK-POT®** slow cooker; stir to blend. Cover; cook on LOW 6 to 8 hours or on HIGH 3 to 4 hours.

Makes 8 servings

Nutrition Information:
Serving Size ½ cup, **Calories** 99, **Total Fat** 2g, **Saturated Fat** 1g, **Protein** 4g, **Carbohydrate** 19g, **Cholesterol** 0mg, **Dietary Fiber** 4g, **Sodium** 187mg

Simmered Napa Cabbage with Dried Apricots (LF) (LS) (V) (GF)

4 cups napa cabbage or green cabbage, cored, cleaned and thinly sliced

1 cup chopped dried apricots

½ cup dry red wine

¼ cup clover honey

2 tablespoons orange juice

Salt and black pepper (optional)

Grated orange peel (optional)

Combine cabbage, apricots, wine, honey and orange juice in **CROCK-POT**® slow cooker; toss to blend. Cover; cook on LOW 5 to 6 hours or on HIGH 2 to 3 hours. Season with salt and pepper, if desired. Garnish with orange peel.

Makes 8 servings

Nutrition Information:
Serving Size ½ cup
Calories 130
Total Fat 0g
Saturated Fat 0g
Protein 2g
Carbohydrate 27g
Cholesterol 0mg
Dietary Fiber 2g
Sodium 10mg

Escalloped Corn Ⓥ

2 tablespoons unsalted butter

½ cup chopped onion

3 tablespoons all-purpose flour

1 cup fat-free (skim) milk

4 cups frozen corn, divided

½ teaspoon salt

½ teaspoon dried thyme

¼ teaspoon black pepper

⅛ teaspoon ground nutmeg

Sprigs fresh thyme (optional)

1. Melt butter in small saucepan over medium heat. Add onion; cook and stir 5 minutes or until tender. Add flour; cook and stir 1 minute. Stir in milk. Bring to a boil; cook and stir 1 minute or until thickened.

2. Place 2 cups corn in food processor or blender; process until coarsely chopped. Combine milk mixture, chopped corn and remaining 2 cups whole corn, salt, dried thyme, pepper and nutmeg in **CROCK-POT**® slow cooker; stir to blend. Cover; cook on LOW 3½ to 4 hours. Garnish with thyme sprigs.

Makes 6 servings

Nutrition Information:
Serving Size about 1 cup
Calories 150
Total Fat 5g
Saturated Fat 3g
Protein 5g
Carbohydrate 23g
Cholesterol 10mg
Dietary Fiber 3g
Sodium 270mg

Coconut-Lime Sweet Potatoes with Walnuts

2½ **pounds sweet potatoes, cut into 1-inch pieces**

1 **cup shredded carrots**

¾ **cup shredded coconut, toasted and divided***

1 **tablespoon unsalted butter, melted**

3 **tablespoons sugar**

½ **teaspoon salt**

⅓ **cup walnuts, toasted, coarsely chopped and divided****

2 **teaspoons grated lime peel**

*To toast coconut, spread evenly on ungreased baking sheet. Toast in preheated 350°F oven 5 to 7 minutes or until light golden brown, stirring occasionally.

**To toast walnuts, spread in single layer in small skillet. Cook and stir over medium heat 1 to 2 minutes or until nuts are lightly browned.

1. Combine sweet potatoes, carrots, ½ cup coconut, butter, sugar and salt in **CROCK-POT**® slow cooker. Cover; cook on LOW 5 to 6 hours. Remove to large bowl.

2. Mash sweet potatoes with potato masher. Stir in 3 tablespoons walnuts and lime peel. Sprinkle each serving with remaining walnuts and coconut.

Makes 8 servings

Nutrition Information:
Serving Size 1⅓ cups, **Calories** 207, **Total Fat** 6g, **Saturated Fat** 2g, **Protein** 3g, **Carbohydrate** 37g, **Cholesterol** 4mg, **Dietary Fiber** 6g, **Sodium** 243mg.

Collard Greens

- 1 **tablespoon olive oil**
- 3 **turkey necks**
- 5 **bunches collard greens, stemmed and chopped**
- 5 **cups reduced-sodium chicken broth**
- 1 **small onion, chopped**
- 2 **cloves garlic, minced**
- 1 **tablespoon apple cider vinegar**
- 1 **teaspoon sugar**
- 1 **teaspoon red pepper flakes**

1. Heat oil in large skillet over medium-high heat. Add turkey necks; cook and stir 3 to 5 minutes or until brown.

2. Combine turkey necks, collard greens, broth, onion and garlic in **CROCK-POT**® slow cooker. Cover; cook on LOW 5 to 6 hours. Remove and discard turkey necks. Stir in vinegar, sugar and red pepper flakes.

Makes 6 servings

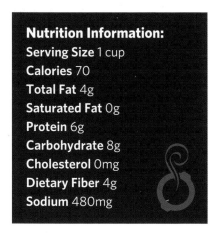

Nutrition Information:
Serving Size 1 cup
Calories 70
Total Fat 4g
Saturated Fat 0g
Protein 6g
Carbohydrate 8g
Cholesterol 0mg
Dietary Fiber 4g
Sodium 480mg

Sweet Potato and Pecan Casserole

 1 **can (40 ounces) sweet potatoes, drained and mashed**

 ½ **cup apple juice**

 4 **tablespoons unsalted butter, melted and divided**

 2 **eggs, beaten**

 ½ **teaspoon salt**

 ½ **teaspoon ground cinnamon**

 ¼ **teaspoon black pepper**

 ⅓ **cup packed brown sugar**

 ¼ **cup chopped pecans**

 2 **tablespoons all-purpose flour**

1. Combine sweet potatoes, apple juice, 2 tablespoons butter, eggs, salt, cinnamon and pepper in large bowl; stir to blend. Place mixture in **CROCK-POT**® slow cooker.

2. Combine brown sugar, pecans, flour and remaining 2 tablespoons butter in small bowl. Spread over sweet potatoes in **CROCK-POT**® slow cooker. Cover; cook on HIGH 3 to 4 hours.

Makes 8 servings

Nutrition Information:
Serving Size ¾ cup
Calories 250
Total Fat 8g
Saturated Fat 3g
Protein 5g
Carbohydrate 43g
Cholesterol 60mg
Dietary Fiber 3g
Sodium 240mg

Asian Golden Barley with Cashews HF V

- **2 tablespoons olive oil**
- **1 cup dry hulled barley, sorted**
- **3 cups reduced-sodium vegetable broth**
- **1 cup chopped celery**
- **1 medium green bell pepper, chopped**
- **1 medium yellow onion, peeled and minced**
- **1 clove garlic, minced**
- **¼ teaspoon black pepper**
- **1 ounce finely chopped lightly salted cashews**

1. Heat oil in large skillet over medium heat. Add barley; cook and stir 10 minutes or until barley is slightly browned. Remove to **CROCK-POT®** slow cooker.

2. Add broth, celery, bell pepper, onion, garlic and black pepper; stir to combine. Cover; cook on LOW 4 to 5 hours or on HIGH 2 to 3 hours or until barley is tender and liquid is absorbed. Top each serving evenly with cashews.

Makes 4 servings

Nutrition Information:
Serving Size 2 cups, **Calories** 310, **Total Fat** 12g, **Saturated Fat** 2g, **Protein** 8g, **Carbohydrate** 45g, **Cholesterol** 0mg, **Dietary Fiber** 11g, **Sodium** 150mg

Orange-Spiced Sweet Potatoes LS V GF

2 pounds sweet potatoes, diced

½ cup packed dark brown sugar

2 tablespoons unsalted butter, cut into small pieces

1 teaspoon ground cinnamon

½ teaspoon ground nutmeg

½ teaspoon grated orange peel

Juice of 1 medium orange

¼ teaspoon salt

1 teaspoon vanilla

Chopped toasted pecans (optional)*

TIP

For a creamy variation, mash potatoes with a potato masher or electric mixer and add ¼ cup milk or whipping cream. Sprinkle with cinnamon-sugar mixture and toasted pecans.

To toast pecans, spread in a single layer in small heavy skillet. Cook and stir over medium heat 1 to 2 minutes or until lightly browned.

Place sweet potatoes, brown sugar, butter, cinnamon, nutmeg, orange peel, orange juice, salt and vanilla in **CROCK-POT**® slow cooker. Cover; cook on LOW 4 hours or on HIGH 2 hours. Sprinkle with pecans before serving, if desired.

Makes 8 servings

Nutrition Information:
Serving Size about ¾ cup
Calories 198
Total Fat 5g
Saturated Fat 2g
Protein 2g
Carbohydrate 38g
Cholesterol 8mg
Dietary Fiber 4g
Sodium 140mg

Lemon Dilled Parsnips and Turnips ⓛⒻ

  4 **turnips, peeled and cut into ½-inch pieces**

  3 **parsnips, cut into ½-inch pieces**

  2 **cups fat-free reduced-sodium chicken broth**

  ¼ **cup chopped green onions**

  ¼ **cup dried dill**

  ¼ **cup lemon juice**

  1 **teaspoon minced garlic**

  ¼ **cup cold water**

  ¼ **cup cornstarch**

1. Combine turnips, parsnips, broth, green onions, dill, lemon juice and garlic in **CROCK-POT**® slow cooker; stir to blend. Cover; cook on LOW 3 to 4 hours or on HIGH 1 to 3 hours.

2. Stir water into cornstarch in small bowl until smooth. Whisk into **CROCK-POT**® slow cooker. Cover; cook on HIGH 15 minutes or until thickened.

Makes 10 servings

Nutrition Information:
Serving Size about ¾ cup
Calories 70
Total Fat 0g
Saturated Fat 0g
Protein 2g
Carbohydrate 16g
Cholesterol 0mg
Dietary Fiber 3g
Sodium 226mg

Barley Risotto with Fennel 🄻🄵 🄷🄵

- **1** cup uncooked pearl barley
- **1** medium fennel bulb, cored and finely diced (about ½ cup)
- **1** carrot, finely chopped
- **1** shallot, finely chopped
- **2** teaspoons ground fennel seed
- **1** clove garlic, minced
- **1** container (32 ounces) reduced-sodium chicken broth
- **1** cup water
- **1½** cups frozen cut green beans
- **½** cup grated Parmesan cheese
- **1** tablespoon grated lemon peel
- **1** teaspoon black pepper

1. Coat inside of **CROCK-POT**® slow cooker with nonstick cooking spray. Combine barley, diced fennel, carrot, shallot, ground fennel and garlic in **CROCK-POT**® slow cooker; stir to blend. Pour in broth and water. Cover; cook on HIGH 3 hours or until barley is tender and risotto is thick and creamy.

2. Turn off heat. Stir green beans, cheese, lemon peel and pepper into risotto. (If risotto appears dry, stir in a few tablespoons of additional water.)

Makes 6 servings

Nutrition Information:
Serving Size about 1½ cups, **Calories** 188, **Total Fat** 3g, **Saturated Fat** 2g, **Protein** 9g, **Carbohydrate** 33g, **Cholesterol** 8mg, **Dietary Fiber** 8g, **Sodium** 205mg

Mexican-Style Spinach ⬤ ⬤ ⬤ ⬤ ⬤

3 **packages (10 ounces *each*) frozen chopped spinach**

1 **tablespoon canola oil**

1 **onion, chopped**

1 **clove garlic, minced**

2 **Anaheim chiles, roasted, peeled and minced***

3 **fresh tomatillos, roasted, husks removed and chopped****

*To roast chiles, heat large heavy skillet over medium-high heat. Add chiles; cook and turn until blackened all over. Place chiles in brown paper bag 2 to 5 minutes. Remove chiles from bag; scrape off charred skin. Cut off top and pull out core. Slice lengthwise; scrape off veins and any remaining seeds with a knife.

**To roast tomatillos, heat large heavy skillet over medium heat. Add tomatillos with papery husks; cook 10 minutes or until husks are brown and interior flesh is soft. Remove and discard husks when cool enough to handle.

Place spinach in **CROCK-POT**® slow cooker. Heat oil in large skillet over medium heat. Add onion and garlic; cook and stir 5 minutes or until onion is tender. Add chiles and tomatillos; cook 3 to 4 minutes. Remove onion mixture to **CROCK-POT**® slow cooker. Cover; cook on LOW 4 to 6 hours.

Makes 6 servings

Nutrition Information:
Serving Size about ¾ cup
Calories 81
Total Fat 3g
Saturated Fat 0g
Protein 6g
Carbohydrate 10g
Cholesterol 0mg
Dietary Fiber 5g
Sodium 107mg

Tarragon Carrots in White Wine

 8 medium carrots, cut into matchsticks

 ½ cup fat-free reduced-sodium chicken broth

 ½ cup dry white wine

 1 tablespoon lemon juice

 1 tablespoon minced fresh tarragon

 2 teaspoons finely chopped green onions

1½ teaspoons chopped fresh Italian parsley

 1 clove garlic, minced

 2 tablespoons melba toast, crushed

 2 tablespoons cold water

1. Combine carrots, broth, wine, lemon juice, tarragon, green onions, parsley and garlic in **CROCK-POT®** slow cooker; stir to blend. Cover; cook on LOW 2½ to 3 hours or on HIGH 1½ to 2 hours.

2. Dissolve toast crumbs in water in small bowl; add to **CROCK-POT®** slow cooker. Cover; cook on LOW 10 minutes or until thickened.

Makes 6 servings

Nutrition Information:
Serving Size about ½ cup
Calories 80
Total Fat 0g
Saturated Fat 0g
Protein 2g
Carbohydrate 16g
Cholesterol 0mg
Dietary Fiber 3g
Sodium 160mg

Roasted Summer Squash with Pine Nuts and Romano Cheese

- 2 tablespoons extra virgin olive oil
- ½ cup chopped yellow onion
- 1 medium red bell pepper, chopped
- 1 clove garlic, minced
- 3 medium zucchini, cut into ½-inch slices
- 3 medium summer squash, cut into ½-inch slices
- ½ cup chopped pine nuts
- ⅓ cup grated Romano cheese
- 1 teaspoon Italian seasoning
- 1 teaspoon salt
- ¼ teaspoon black pepper
- 1 tablespoon unsalted butter, cubed

1. Heat oil in large skillet over medium-high heat. Add onion, bell pepper and garlic; cook and stir 10 minutes or until onion is softened. Remove to **CROCK-POT**® slow cooker. Add zucchini and squash; toss lightly.

2. Combine pine nuts, cheese, Italian seasoning, salt and pepper in small bowl; stir to blend. Fold half of cheese mixture into squash in **CROCK-POT**® slow cooker. Sprinkle remaining cheese mixture on top. Dot cheese with butter. Cover; cook on LOW 4 to 6 hours.

Makes 8 servings

Nutrition Information:
Serving Size about ¾ cup, **Calories** 150, **Total Fat** 12g, **Saturated Fat** 3g, **Protein** 4g, **Carbohydrate** 8g, **Cholesterol** 5mg, **Dietary Fiber** 2g, **Sodium** 370mg

Orange-Spice Glazed Carrots 🄻🄵 🄻🄂 🅅 🄶🄵

   1 **package (32 ounces) baby carrots**

  ½ **cup packed light brown sugar**

  ½ **cup orange juice**

   1 **tablespoon unsalted butter**

  ¾ **teaspoon ground cinnamon**

  ¼ **teaspoon ground nutmeg**

  ¼ **cup cold water**

   2 **tablespoons cornstarch**

1. Combine carrots, brown sugar, orange juice, butter, cinnamon and nutmeg in **CROCK-POT**® slow cooker. Cover; cook on LOW 3½ to 4 hours or until carrots are crisp-tender. Spoon carrots into large serving bowl.

2. Turn **CROCK-POT**® slow cooker to HIGH. Stir water into cornstarch in small bowl until smooth. Whisk into **CROCK-POT**® slow cooker. Cover; cook on HIGH 15 minutes or until thickened. Spoon sauce evenly over carrots.

Makes 6 servings

Nutrition Information:
Serving Size about ¾ cup
Calories 179
Total Fat 2g
Saturated Fat 1g
Protein 2g
Carbohydrate 39g
Cholesterol 5mg
Dietary Fiber 4g
Sodium 6mg

Herbed Fall Vegetables LF HF

- **2** medium Yukon Gold potatoes, cut into ½-inch pieces
- **2** medium sweet potatoes, cut into ½-inch pieces
- **3** parsnips, cut into ½-inch pieces
- **1** medium bulb of fennel, sliced and cut into ½-inch pieces
- **1** cup fat-free reduced-sodium chicken broth
- **¾** cup chopped fresh Italian parsley
- **2** tablespoons unsalted butter, cubed
- **1** tablespoon salt
- **½** teaspoon black pepper

Combine potatoes, parsnips, fennel, broth, parsley, butter, salt and pepper in **CROCK-POT**® slow cooker. Cover; cook on LOW 4½ hours or on HIGH 3 hours, stirring halfway through cooking time.

Makes 6 servings

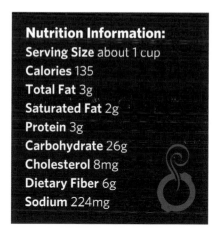

Nutrition Information:
Serving Size about 1 cup
Calories 135
Total Fat 3g
Saturated Fat 2g
Protein 3g
Carbohydrate 26g
Cholesterol 8mg
Dietary Fiber 6g
Sodium 224mg

Lemon-Mint Red Potatoes Ⓥ ⒼⒻ

- 2 pounds new red potatoes
- 3 tablespoons extra virgin olive oil
- 1 teaspoon salt
- ¾ teaspoon Greek seasoning or dried oregano
- ¼ teaspoon garlic powder
- ¼ teaspoon black pepper
- ¼ cup chopped fresh mint, divided
- 2 tablespoons lemon juice
- 1 tablespoon unsalted butter
- 1 teaspoon grated lemon peel

TIP

It's easy to prepare these potatoes ahead of time. Simply follow the recipe and then turn off the heat. Let it stand at room temperature for up to 2 hours. You may reheat or serve the potatoes at room temperature.

1. Coat inside of **CROCK-POT**® slow cooker with nonstick cooking spray. Combine potatoes and oil in **CROCK-POT**® slow cooker; toss gently to coat. Sprinkle with salt, Greek seasoning, garlic powder and pepper. Cover; cook on LOW 7 hours or on HIGH 4 hours.

2. Add 2 tablespoons mint, lemon juice, butter and lemon peel; stir until butter is melted. Cover; cook on HIGH 15 minutes. Garnish with remaining 2 tablespoons mint.

Makes 6 servings

Nutrition Information:
Serving Size about ½ cup potatoes, **Calories** 190, **Total Fat** 9g, **Saturated Fat** 2g, **Protein** 3g, **Carbohydrate** 25g, **Cholesterol** 5mg, **Dietary Fiber** 3g, **Sodium** 400mg

Supper Squash Medley LF HF

2 **butternut squash, peeled, seeded and diced (about 4 cups)**

1 **can (28 ounces) diced tomatoes**

1 **can (15 ounces) corn, drained**

2 **medium onions, chopped**

2 **medium green bell peppers, chopped**

2 **teaspoons minced garlic**

2 **mild green chile peppers, chopped***

1 **cup fat-free reduced-sodium chicken broth**

½ **teaspoon black pepper**

1 **can (6 ounces) tomato paste**

Chile peppers can sting and irritate the skin, so wear rubber gloves when handling peppers and do not touch your eyes.

1. Combine squash, tomatoes, corn, onions, bell peppers, garlic, green chiles, broth, salt and black pepper in **CROCK-POT**® slow cooker; stir to blend. Cover; cook on LOW 6 hours.

2. Turn **CROCK-POT**® slow cooker to HIGH. Remove about ½ cup cooking liquid to small bowl; stir in tomato paste. Whisk into **CROCK-POT**® slow cooker; stir to blend. Cover; cook on HIGH 15 minutes or until mixture is thickened and heated through.

Makes 8 servings

Nutrition Information:
Serving Size about 1¼ cups, **Calories** 140, **Total Fat** 1g, **Saturated Fat** 0g, **Protein** 4g, **Carbohydrate** 30g, **Cholesterol** 0mg, **Dietary Fiber** 7g, **Sodium** 430mg

Red Cabbage and Apples ⓛⓕ ⓛⓢ ⓥ ⓖⓕ

1 **small head red cabbage, cored and thinly sliced**

1 **large apple, peeled and grated**

¾ **cup sugar**

½ **cup red wine vinegar**

1 **teaspoon ground cloves**

Fresh apple slices (optional)

Combine cabbage, grated apples, sugar, vinegar and cloves in **CROCK-POT®** slow cooker; stir to blend. Cover; cook on HIGH 6 hours, stirring halfway through cooking time. Garnish with apple slices.

Makes 6 servings

Nutrition Information:
Serving Size about ¾ cup
Calories 147
Total Fat 0g
Saturated Fat 0g
Protein 1g
Carbohydrate 37g
Cholesterol 0mg
Dietary Fiber 3g
Sodium 29mg

Green Bean Casserole ⓥ

2 packages (10 ounces *each*) frozen green beans

1 can (10¾ ounces) reduced-sodium condensed cream of mushroom soup, undiluted

1 tablespoon chopped fresh Italian parsley

1 tablespoon chopped roasted red peppers

1 teaspoon dried sage

½ teaspoon salt

½ teaspoon black pepper

¼ teaspoon ground nutmeg

½ cup toasted slivered almonds*

*To toast almonds, spread in single layer in small skillet. Cook and stir over medium heat 1 to 2 minutes or until nuts are lightly browned.

Combine beans, soup, parsley, red peppers, sage, salt, black pepper and nutmeg in **CROCK-POT®** slow cooker. Cover; cook on LOW 3 to 4 hours. Sprinkle each serving evenly with almonds.

Makes 6 servings

Nutrition Information:
Serving Size about ¾ cup
Calories 91
Total Fat 7g
Saturated Fat 1g
Protein 4g
Carbohydrate 13g
Cholesterol 2mg
Dietary Fiber 4g
Sodium 221mg

Quinoa and Vegetable Medley

2 medium sweet potatoes, cut into ½-inch-thick slices

1 medium eggplant, cut into ½-inch cubes

1 large green bell pepper, sliced

1 medium tomato, cut into wedges

1 small onion, cut into wedges

½ teaspoon salt

¼ teaspoon ground red pepper

¼ teaspoon black pepper

1 cup uncooked quinoa

2 cups fat-free reduced-sodium vegetable broth

2 cloves garlic, minced

½ teaspoon dried thyme

¼ teaspoon dried marjoram

1. Coat inside of **CROCK-POT**® slow cooker with nonstick cooking spray. Combine sweet potatoes, eggplant, bell pepper, tomato, onion, salt, ground red pepper and black pepper in **CROCK-POT**® slow cooker; toss to coat.

2. Place quinoa in strainer; rinse well. Add quinoa to vegetable mixture in **CROCK-POT**® slow cooker. Stir in broth, garlic, thyme and marjoram. Cover; cook on LOW 5 hours or on HIGH 2½ hours or until quinoa is tender and broth is absorbed.

Makes 6 servings

Nutrition Information:
Serving Size 1¼ cups, **Calories** 193, **Total Fat** 2g, **Saturated Fat** 1g, **Protein** 6g, **Carbohydrate** 40g, **Cholesterol** 0mg, **Dietary Fiber** 6g, **Sodium** 194mg

Mashed Rutabagas and Potatoes 🅛🄵 🅛🅂 🆅 🄶🄵

2 pounds rutabagas, peeled and cut into ½-inch pieces

1 pound potatoes, cut into ½-inch pieces

½ cup low-fat (1%) milk

½ teaspoon ground nutmeg

2 tablespoons chopped fresh Italian parsley

Sprigs fresh Italian parsley (optional)

1. Place rutabagas and potatoes in **CROCK-POT**® slow cooker; add enough water to cover vegetables. Cover; cook on LOW 6 hours or on HIGH 3 hours. Remove vegetables to large bowl using slotted spoon. Discard cooking liquid.

2. Mash vegetables with potato masher. Stir in milk, nutmeg and chopped parsley until blended. Garnish with parsley sprigs.

Makes 8 servings

Nutrition Information:
Serving Size 1⅓ cups
Calories 93
Total Fat 1g
Saturated Fat 1g
Protein 3g
Carbohydrate 20g
Cholesterol 1mg
Dietary Fiber 3g
Sodium 30mg

Sunshine Squash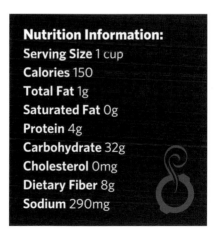

- 1 **butternut squash (about 2 pounds), seeded and diced**
- 1 **can (about 15 ounces) corn, drained**
- 1 **can (about 14 ounces) no-salt-added diced tomatoes**
- 1 **onion, coarsely chopped**
- 1 **green bell pepper, cut into 1-inch pieces**
- ½ **cup fat-free reduced-sodium chicken broth**
- 1 **mild green chile pepper, coarsely chopped**
- 1 **clove garlic, minced**
- ¼ **teaspoon black pepper**
- 1 **tablespoon plus 1½ teaspoons tomato paste**

1. Combine squash, corn, tomatoes, onion, bell pepper, broth, green chile, garlic and black pepper in **CROCK-POT®** slow cooker. Cover; cook on LOW 6 hours.

2. Remove ¼ cup cooking liquid to small bowl; stir in tomato paste. Whisk into **CROCK-POT®** slow cooker. Cover; cook on LOW 30 minutes or until mixture is slightly thickened and heated through.

Makes 6 servings

Nutrition Information:
Serving Size 1 cup
Calories 150
Total Fat 1g
Saturated Fat 0g
Protein 4g
Carbohydrate 32g
Cholesterol 0mg
Dietary Fiber 8g
Sodium 290mg

Lemon-Mint Red Potatoes (page 238)

METRIC CONVERSION CHART

VOLUME MEASUREMENTS (dry)

1/8 teaspoon = 0.5 mL
1/4 teaspoon = 1 mL
1/2 teaspoon = 2 mL
3/4 teaspoon = 4 mL
1 teaspoon = 5 mL
1 tablespoon = 15 mL
2 tablespoons = 30 mL
1/4 cup = 60 mL
1/3 cup = 75 mL
1/2 cup = 125 mL
2/3 cup = 150 mL
3/4 cup = 175 mL
1 cup = 250 mL
2 cups = 1 pint = 500 mL
3 cups = 750 mL
4 cups = 1 quart = 1 L

VOLUME MEASUREMENTS (fluid)

1 fluid ounce (2 tablespoons) = 30 mL
4 fluid ounces (1/2 cup) = 125 mL
8 fluid ounces (1 cup) = 250 mL
12 fluid ounces (1 1/2 cups) = 375 mL
16 fluid ounces (2 cups) = 500 mL

WEIGHTS (mass)

1/2 ounce = 15 g
1 ounce = 30 g
3 ounces = 90 g
4 ounces = 120 g
8 ounces = 225 g
10 ounces = 285 g
12 ounces = 360 g
16 ounces = 1 pound = 450 g

DIMENSIONS

1/16 inch = 2 mm
1/8 inch = 3 mm
1/4 inch = 6 mm
1/2 inch = 1.5 cm
3/4 inch = 2 cm
1 inch = 2.5 cm

OVEN TEMPERATURES

250°F = 120°C
275°F = 140°C
300°F = 150°C
325°F = 160°C
350°F = 180°C
375°F = 190°C
400°F = 200°C
425°F = 220°C
450°F = 230°C

BAKING PAN SIZES

Utensil	Size in Inches/Quarts	Metric Volume	Size in Centimeters
Baking or Cake Pan (square or rectangular)	8×8×2	2 L	20×20×5
	9×9×2	2.5 L	23×23×5
	12×8×2	3 L	30×20×5
	13×9×2	3.5 L	33×23×5
Loaf Pan	8×4×3	1.5 L	20×10×7
	9×5×3	2 L	23×13×7
Round Layer Cake Pan	8×1½	1.2 L	20×4
	9×1½	1.5 L	23×4
Pie Plate	8×1¼	750 mL	20×3
	9×1¼	1 L	23×3
Baking Dish or Casserole	1 quart	1 L	—
	1½ quart	1.5 L	—
	2 quart	2 L	—